T0171610

LUCK O THE IRISH

VIRGINIA JARBOE RN

WestBow
PRESS
A DIVISION OF THOMAS NELSON

WestBow Press books may be ordered through booksellers or by contacting:

WestBow Press
A Division of Thomas Nelson
1663 Liberty Drive
Bloomington, IN 47403
www.westbowpress.com
1-(866) 928-1240

ISBN: 978-1-4497-4476-2 (sc)
ISBN: 978-1-4497-4475-5 (e)

Library of Congress Control Number: 2012907934

Printed in the United States of America

WestBow Press rev. date: 06/06/2012

A fictional story based on a true story of a schizophrenic man and his wild obsessions

CHAPTER ONE

Frightened

"WHERE ARE WE GOING?" A desperate little voice asked. The boy was barely two. Bound hand and foot with old tattered pieces of faded water ski rope, he squirmed to get loose while lying on his side on the vinyl covered back seat of a trashed out wannabe suped up 1965 Impala.

"Shut up and keep still!" the young man with shaggy long hair and a receding hairline snapped back to him, as he nervously looked back briefly at the boy from the front seat. Then, spinning his head back forward, the driver glanced quickly into the rear view mirror at the car on his rear and pressed harder onto the accelerator of the car. His tattered shirt, half buttoned up with sleeves rolled up his arms, became a collection garment for stinky sweat. Speeding forward, weaving around one car, then another, he cut through the late night traffic on Interstate 15, heading west toward Palm Desert on a long, hot stretch of the freeway in southern California in the dead of the summer's heat. The old, stale, musty odor of the vehicle exaggerated itself in the heat. He couldn't lose the car chasing him, but wouldn't give up trying.

"He must be taking him back to his house... the psycho, mad idiot..." the private investigator said mumbling through his clinched teeth, as he plunged his foot harder onto the gas pedal in his unassuming well kept 1969 Ford Fairlane. Though big and tall, the investigator kept himself fairly stealth. In his profession, it became necessary to be strong and fit. Struggling to catch up with the Impala, he then spoke loudly and clearly, punching out the words to himself through his sweaty face, "I can-not be-lieve- it!" The investigator continued while looking amazed at his speedometer. "That crazy man is driving a hun-dred miles an ho-ur!" He snapped his dropped jaw closed and then took a deep breath as he pressed harder onto the accelerator, taking it up to 110 miles per hour. "He's gonna kill the kid! I've got to stop him!" He spit out the words, "Jesus, God help me," as he looked disgustingly ahead at the Impala.

The boy began to cry, "Daddy, I'm scared!" as urine dripped through his soaked diaper and clothes and onto the seat of the car, puddling under his side. He could hear the sound of the engine rumbling and felt the vibrations it made. His dad had dressed him in his blue Osh Kosh B' Gosh jean overalls with a crayon red tee shirt. He'd had all of the boy's clothes stuffed in a box at his apartment the whole nine months he'd had the boy with him. The boy's frightened eyes drifted downward, catching a glimpse of his stuffed, worn out Alf toy, buried in a pile of empty soda cans and the scraps from the ski rope on the floor in front of him. The Alf toy was slightly under the passenger seat and impossible to reach, especially with the boy's hands tied up at his back. He stared blankly at his Alf, wishing he could run away with it to somewhere far, far from his car. He momentarily flashed onto the happy times he always escaped to while sitting in front of the television watching the Alf show, back when his mommy and daddy were home, happy, and all was well... so his young mind thought. Wondering for a moment, where that life went, the boy snapped back to reality when the car took a sudden jerk while passing another vehicle on the road.

"Don't worry," his dad began in a slow, controlled voice, "we'll be home soon, son, and everything will be OK."

It had been just over twenty four hours since they'd been able to stop and eat. Earlier, Richard, a fully American bred Caucasian, had known he was being followed by someone for days, but wasn't sure just who it was. It had been getting more and more noticeable, and then straight up scary at a particular time while he was in a grocery store, trying to obtain some food for his son and himself. He had managed to slip out of the investigator's sight in the snack food isle while ducking out of the store. The boy and he were both hungry and though he was acting in desperation in his attempt to escape, Richard still cared enough to know he needed to feed his son. Unfortunately for Richard, he had to run into the parking lot from the grocery store, while dragging the little boy along by the arm, telling the boy they had to go and leaving behind his only opportunity to get some food. Richard jumped into the driver's seat of the car, tossing the boy onto the passenger's seat and sped off down the street.

Then luckily for him, not more than a mile down the road, he spotted a brand new white and green colored gas station on a corner. Taking advantage of the moment to fill his tank, he swerved into a perfect spot in front of the only available pump. He quickly got out of the car and opened the door of the tank and shoved in the gas nozzle.

Alone inside the car the boy climbed over the front seat and onto the back seat. He stood himself up, and then began staring out the window at his dad. Tears fell from the boy's eyes as he watched his father fill the gas tank. He could hear the chugging of the fluid going into the car and smell the caustic fumes it spilled into the air. His dad never looked his direction, just back down the street where they had just come from. He then watched his dad briskly walk into the station. Not realizing he would only be gone for a few minutes to pay for the gas, he began screaming and crying while staring into the entrance of the shiny white and Kelly- green trimmed gas station.

Immediately, when his dad returned and saw the boy standing there crying, he reached into the back of the car and shook his son, demanding he be quiet and forcing him to sit down. Angrily, he ran around to the trunk of the car and opened it. After digging through a collection of trash and greasy car parts, he found some old fluorescent orange ski rope, shredded in some parts and stained with black grease. He pulled it out, quickly wound it up and threw it into the back seat of the car. "Stay there!" he commanded his son, pushing him down onto the pile of rope. Pointing firmly at the boy, he snapped, "Now, sit down and don't move!"

Once again, Richard sped off in his car. Agitated and scared, he wasn't sure where he was going; he just knew he had to go. It wasn't long before the boy began climbing up onto the seat again. Even more irate than before, Richard swung the car over to the edge of the road, and threw the driver's door open. He got out and angrily opened the boy's door. "Damn you boy!" he spat red faced. He grabbed his son by the arm, asking him, "Why are you disobeying me child?" He picked up the old salvaged ski rope and pulled the boy's legs down hard together and began tying up his ankles. "Now look what you made me have to do!" He bound the wrists after the ankles, shaking as he nervously made the knots. Sweat dripped from his forehead down onto his lips as he spattered, "Never disobey me again!"

It was getting very late now, on this hot, muggy summer night. The distressed child had fallen into a dead sleep, still bound up on the back seat. The smell of the old urine began to permeate the inside of the car. Richard had been driving all day and now deep into the night and he was getting very tired. Almost delirious, he began to wonder, "Who in the world could that guy be who's following me?" Then he speculated, "It has to be undercover cops. It has to be! But," he rationalized, "this is my kid," he continued in his warped mind, "I can do whatever I want with him."

Just then, the Fairlane gained speed and pulled up to the driver's side of the Richard's Impala, shaking him back to reality. "What am I gonna do?" Richard panicked. He turned his head briefly to see who the driver of the Fairlane was, but in the dark, couldn't make out the face. He pressed even harder onto the accelerator, and with his foot down as hard as he could press, he pushed ahead of the investigator's car.

"This guy's a mad man!" the investigator mumbled under his breath as he too pressed as hard as he could onto his gas pedal. "I gotta get him!"

Both cars raced down the long, seemingly never ending road for miles, side by side. Each of them took the opportunity to stare into the other's car whenever they could see in enough to give an angry look into the other's eyes. Suddenly Richard took a glance at his gas gage and noticed he was on empty. There was no place to pull off the freeway and no exit in sight. Moments later, the Impala began to slowly lose speed. "No! Damn! This can't happen!" Richard exclaimed.

"Thank you Jesus!" the investigator cried out slowing with the mad man's car, keeping his car just inches from the Impala. "You're not getting away from me now you psycho crazy man!"

Richard panicked, slammed on his brakes, swerving to the edge of the road, with the tail of his vehicle still halfway into the freeway. Quickly, the investigator followed, braking also, struggling to keep from hitting the Impala and parked close behind it.

As soon as both cars had completely stopped, the investigator flung his car door open and ran to the Impala. He opened the back door and snatched the little boy right out of the car.

With not a second to spare, Richard got out of his car and yanked on his son's legs, trying to break him loose from the investigator's grip, as the investigator headed to his vehicle. "Who are you?" Richard demanded. "Give me my son back!"

The investigator had the boy in a football hold and wasn't about to let go of him. As fast as he could, he swooped the boy away and placed him in the passenger seat of his car, never saying a word to Richard.

Richard tried to reach into the Fairlane to get his son, but the investigator let go of the boy, threw out his arm, and boldly shoved Richard right out of his doorway while smashing a stack of legal papers into his chest at the same time. Richard landed into the middle of the freeway onto his butt. With papers floating around him and onto the road, he sat stunned with his legs open and his heels dug into the cement. His blue jeans had fallen half way down his butt as he sat staring in disbelief as to what had just happened.

The investigator pulled his car door closed and in one fleeting moment drove away, swooshing the paperwork all around Richard, never looking back.

When Richard came to, he saw the papers getting further away. He reached out onto the side of the highway, groping around in the dark with his arms flailing wildly, shaky and desperate for them, gathering the pile into a wad.

"It's gonna be OK, Joshua," the investigator said softly to the boy. "I'm gonna get you back to your mommy now." Joshua laid there, still bound, frightened.

Chapter Two

Race Car

The young man smiled as he spun off in his Impala once again. It was mid afternoon. He looked out the dusty windshield proudly observing the bold, wide black stripe down the center of the front hood of his car, spanning two-thirds of the dented and faded tan color. He had just painted it on. It went from the heavy, crooked back bumper, covering the rusted chrome, all of the way up the back hood, skipping the rear window, up onto the top, past the windshield and over to the front hood and bumper! "Wow! What a hot race car!" he thought proudly to himself, taking in a whiff of the familiar old car stale odor it possessed.

He didn't think anything of how unacceptable his vehicle looked. As a matter of fact, the passersby who stared oddly at him were, to him, merely admirers of his *race car*. He raced around town, heading nowhere in particular, just forward and through as many public places as he could hit in the quaint little town of Bennett Valley, near the wine country in northern California. It was 1998. His 1968 Impala would have been a beautiful 30 year old classic by now, had it been truly restored. But, the long, flat hood was now full of dents and rust spots, much of it covered in a sloppily painted black stripe. The metal stripping along one side was missing, leaving only little holes in the side where it had been attached. The rear view mirror on the passenger side was long gone, but the driver's side mirror worked like new. He liked reaching his hand out when the window was rolled open to adjust it while he was driving. Whether he had anything to look at or not, he often checked the mirror. He was proud of his "two door, automatic, eight cylinder race car," as he put it.

Josh had saved two hundred dollars from jobs he managed to get paid for around the neighborhood. He mowed lawns and even washed cars to earn the money. He had spotted the Impala parked on the roadside with a sign that said, 'For sale, $800.00.' He knew instinctively that the car belonged to him. After convincing his parents to kick in the rest, he managed to buy his first car.

Briefly, the young man snapped out of his day dreaming with the fleeting thought, "I hope I have enough gas to get me home." He took a look at the gas gauge, noting the red line stuck way past the "E". Just then the car started to skip and putt. "Damn! It's gonna die!" He pulled over to the side of the road and parked the car. After getting out, he stood by the side of the road and stared at it saying, "Why did you have to go and do that?" He kicked the front driver's side wheel and he began walking in the direction of his home, leaving his *prized car* behind.

Only sixteen, Joshua had barely gotten his driver's license. His mother reluctantly signed for him, but only because of his constant persistence in asking to have it. He knew his way around town well, as he had lived in the area since he was two. There was one freeway going through the nearby city of Santa Rosa; highway 101. Whenever he got the chance, he would hop onto it so he could speed in his *race car*. After a mile or two, he'd pull onto the off ramp of the highway then get right back on going the opposite direction.

"Joshua, why did you drive your car when it was nearly empty?" his mother asked, after he returned home late that evening. His mother, Vickie was a cheerful person by nature, though very excitable. "Didn't you check the gas gauge before you left?" The Norwegian ancestry gave way to her straight forward questioning in most circumstances. Though, usually, it took a lot to get her truly upset. Nearly forty years old and brunette, Vickie had a few extra pounds collected around her waistline from bearing five children. She dressed comfortably, wearing stretch pants and tee shirts most of the time.

"Duh! You can't race a car if it is full!"

"What?" his mother exclaimed.

"You know all race car drivers have to drive empty cars."

"Whatever. I'm not paying to get it towed back. If you want that car, you'll have to go get it yourself!"

"You always help the other kids, why can't you help me?"

His mother sat exhausted. All afternoon she had worried about where he was, calling school mates of his, trying to locate him. She shook her head, looking downward. "Why doesn't he understand?" she thought. So many years of misbehavior from this child, she grew weary of his antics. There seemed to be no getting better. Mostly, things just kept getting worse.

Vickie had been married for fifteen years to her good Mormon husband, Matthew. A six foot tall, fairly fit man in his mid forties, Matthew was mild mannered and generally easy going. His rough complexion and rugged beard didn't accurately tell of his gentle countenance. Together they'd had four more children since Joshua. Matthew had willingly taken on the decision to parent Josh shortly after the kidnapping from his natural father, Richard, had been resolved.

Vickie's new found faith in Mormonism at the time just after the kidnapping had her believing that her Heavenly Father would work out the details of Josh's young, traumatized life and she vowed to herself to never worry about the consequences of adding more children to the family she had started.

Vickie never forgot, though, the moment Joshua was returned to her. It seemed as though those nine months without her son was a million years. She had been in her early twenties at the time and thoroughly loved her son.

She had prayed every day and night for his return. She spent all she had hiring the private investigator who found and returned Joshua to her. When the phone call came that Joshua was safe with him that frightful summer night on the desert highway, Vickie went out and bought the biggest and most fragrant candle she could find. It had been a tradition she'd created as a child, to light a candle when something special happened in her life. Perhaps, she'd first come up with the idea from candles on her birthday cake. This time, it was the most incredible reason to feel special. The God of the heavens was returning her child to her! The off white colored candle was about a foot high and very strongly vanilla scented. She found a spot on her mantle where she immediately lit the candle. The fragrance of vanilla lingered in her home for weeks. It burned half way down, waiting for Joshua and then continued to burn long after his arrival home.

Though well aware of the painful first two years Joshua had suffered from his obsessive, alcoholic father, Vickie kept the faith that love and care would make everything work out over time with his life. It repulsed her to even think of Richard and all that he had imposed onto their innocent little child at such a young age, so she closed that door in her mind, and resolved to not think about her ex-husband ever again. Now, she was married to the *perfect man*.

Together Vickie and Matthew began raising Joshua along with their growing family. There was a lot of extended family, leaving Joshua with many cousins to visit on holidays and special occasions. His life was full of family, church, and unfortunately, punishments. He was a child who could push the envelope at every given opportunity, always demanding attention and needing affirmation. His mother tried hard to be fair, but as it seemed, her other children were simply well behaved. Joshua grew jealous and began throwing fits early on.

With his wheels gone and no way of paying to get the car towed back home, Josh lay irritated on his bed in his room. "I didn't even get the chance to show the others my racing stripe," he thought. He preferred referring to his brothers and sisters as *the others*. He grew increasingly annoyed. Then he sarcastically mumbled to himself, "The others always get all the attention". He continued, thinking about his parents, "They don't care about me. They never did!" Filled with resentfulness he sprung off his bed, walked toward the door swinging it open and yelled out to his mom, "I hate you!" then slammed his door shut.

The evening passed and the next morning brought hope for a better day. Vickie hurriedly poured a bowl full of Lucky Charms into each of the kid's breakfast bowls, as they sat around the table waiting to be fed. She loved the large space the kitchen provided her, as she could get so much done while the kids were eating. She began to pour the milk for each of them when Josh stopped her at his, with his hand covering his bowl saying, "Don't, I like it dry." So Vickie skipped his bowl and poured the milk into the other bowls for each of the rest of the children.

Josh began to pick out the dry, colored marshmallows from his bowl and laid them out in a line onto the table. The other kids watched quietly as they ate their sweet, crunchy cereal. "This is a moon in heaven and this is a diamond jewel" he explained to Camden, only five and the youngest in the family. He pointed to the yellow moon and the blue diamond. Camden looked wide eyed, with his bright blue eyes staring at the little line of yummy charms that weren't getting eaten quite yet. Josh observed his thoughts, "want one?" he asked. Camden nodded his little blonde head and Josh scooped them up and dumped them onto the boy's cereal.

"Quit playing with your food, Josh. Just eat it, would you?" Vickie spat out.

Josh giggled and picked out the cereal pieces one by one, eating them as he demonstrated his defiance in front of his siblings.

After wiping the counters and placing dishes from the night before into the dishwasher, Vickie went for the white phone mounted onto the wall. She picked up the hand piece tugging on its spring like cord which was attached to the wall mounted phone as she walked away with it held against her ear. Then, spotting a couple oat cereal pieces on the floor next to Camden, she knelt down to pick them up. Keeping her eye on the kids as they finished up their breakfast, she stepped back to dial the phone number to the new seventeen year old babysitter that she and Matthew had just recruited from their church.

The babysitter knew the kids from their involvement at church, but hadn't babysat for them before. "Can you just come over for a couple of hours?" Vickie said, twirling the stretched out cord between her fingers. In her nervousness, she stood with her legs crossed as she gazed off to the side, away from her children. "I have some things I need to do down at the church," she said slowly, knowing subconsciously it was a bad idea to leave the children with a babysitter. "It shouldn't take me long."

Josh listened as she made the arrangements. It was common for his mother to utilize a babysitter, though he was old enough to babysit *the others* himself. She didn't trust him, though- and rightfully so.

"It's mine!" cried Karley, his seven year old youngest sister. Karley was the outspoken one. She rarely held back her feelings. She was tall for her age and a little chubby. She liked to change her outfits often, making her hair style match the outfit. This day she was wearing a bright pink polka dotted blouse with hot pink shorts. Her tummy poked out just under the hem of her islet trimmed blouse. Her hair was up in a sophisticated looking bun, while she insisted she was a princess.

This just made the teasing more fun. Joshua dangled Karley's doll in front of her as she cried out for it, "Gimmie back my baby!" Walking with it out of living room sliding door, he threw it over the two story high balcony, watching it fall down the hillside slope and into the overgrown plants and weeds. And, as if to accentuate the action, Fluffy, their long white haired Persian cat quickly jumped off the balcony, onto the tree and ran down the tree after the doll.

With a big smile on his face, feeling like a conqueror in his little kingdom called home, he spoke down to his little sister, "Now, you go get it if you want it so bad... princess!"

The young teenager babysitting didn't know what to do about the situation. Karley was crying. Camden was watching and trembling, his eyes filling with tears the other kids withdrew to the kitchen, avoiding the whole situation. She looked at Josh and said, "you're mean! Ya know that?"

"So what!" He quickly responded with a sarcastic tone. "What are you gonna do about it- spank me?" He stood directly across from her, arms on hips, matching her size. Then laughing, he began to poke at Camden, "look at the little baby. Are you gonna cry too?" Camden was afraid of Joshua and always began crying when he saw Josh picking on the other children.

The babysitter reached over to Camden, holding his little hand and pulling him close to her side safely.

"You're just like the rest of them!" Josh said rudely to the teen. "It's always the little babies first."

"I'm gonna tell your mom when she gets back," the teen said sternly to Josh. "Just leave the kids alone!"

Karley was crying loudly, reaching her arms around the sitter's hips. "Shhh Karley, it's gonna be all right. We'll get your dolly back," the babysitter said with her voice trembling holding back tears of her own. She perceived the deep, disturbing family dynamics. Little Camden clung to the baby sitter's other side, shaking, with tears falling down his round, soft little cheeks.

The baby sitter began to wonder what this kid her age was really capable of, and it scared her. She moved the other kids into the living room, away from Joshua, hoping to get them calmed down.

But, as life would have it, Josh followed them to the living room, nagging each of his siblings into hysterics. Just as he walked into the room, he let off a rancid smelling fart. "Ohh," he said with relief in his voice, "that felt good!" With that, he began rubbing his belly.

Not knowing what to do, the babysitter turned on the TV and plopped down onto the couch, trying to ignore Josh. She pulled Camden and Karley close to her on each side. The other two children moved into the living room with her, sitting on the floor at her feet.

At that moment, Vickie walked in. "I'm home!" Then immediately following was, "Ugh!" She waved the smell away from her nose. She noticed Joshua smiling proudly in return.

"Oh, good! You're home!" the babysitter blurted out with her quivering voice as she bolted up off the couch. Camden and Karley quickly ran to their mother, as the other two stood to their feet.

Vickie quickly turned her attention to the sitter. "What happened?" she asked, observing the tension.

"It's Joshua. He keeps picking on the other kids. He threw Karley's doll over the balcony. He makes them cry and I don't know what to do!" She paused, as she began making her way toward the front door, now beginning to get the drift of the odor Josh passed, "pee-yew, it stinks! I've gotta go." She continued, shaking her head in disgust. "I'm sorry."

The other two kids joined their mother. "Josh, go to your room!" she demanded, pointing in the direction of his room down the hall. Vickie placed her arms on the shoulders of her children, drawing them into her, turning her attention to them. Josh walked slowly to his room, with a smirk on his face, staring each one of his siblings down as he passed them. When he reached his room, he slammed the door shut, and then with a devious smirk on his face, reopened it slightly. He held his ear to the opening as he listened to the conversation in the living room.

"I'm so sorry about this," Vickie said with a shaky voice to the sitter. She stepped away from the kids and walked toward the front door, where the sitter stood, with one hand on the knob. "Joshua can be such a problem sometimes." As if rehearsed, she continued, "Let me pay you a little extra for your difficulty here." Vickie reached into her purse and pulled out some dollar bills she had piled together with an extra twenty, knowing ahead of time it would be necessary and put the handful of dollars into the babysitter's hand. She opened the door for her with total embarrassment. The sitter looked at her sadly and walked away without saying another word. Vickie quickly closed the door behind her, pausing a moment with her forehead resting on the door. "Why, Heavenly Father?" she whispered to herself.

"Joshua, come out, we need to talk!" Vickie demanded, as she turned from the front door, redirection her attention. The other children went into the living room and sat on the couch and continued to watch the television, trying to stay out of the way, as they had done so many times prior whenever Josh was in trouble.

"What for?" he replied slowly, with an evil sort of smile on his face, as he returned to the kitchen.

"Why do you have to do that, Josh? You know she'll never come back now! So, why do you keep doing that to us? What am I gonna do now?' Vickie stressfully questioned. "That was the last person we knew of to babysit. You've scared them all off!"

Joshua interrupted, "You always blame me for everything! What about *the others*. How come they never get in trouble? Huh? It's always me you're yelling at!" poking his finger firmly into his own chest.

Vickie continued her frustrated train of thought, "Joshua, you stir it up. You get them crying. You make everyone mad!" His mother couldn't stop the angry blaming. "You're so difficult. Don't you understand? We're just trying to have a happy family! We don't need you getting everyone upset all of the time! You're just like your father!" Vickie gasped, covering her mouth. She suddenly realized what she was saying. It felt like she was speaking to the identical personality of the man she once married, many years ago.

"I wish I was never born!" Josh said, perceiving her thoughts. "I wish you'd give me back to my *real* father!" He cried out. "At least he would only have *me* to take care of and none of these other brats!"

"Fine, go back to him. See how you like it there." Again, she couldn't believe herself. She let the words out that she had promised herself she would never say. Then, a flash of the moment, when he was returned to her after the kidnapping, crossed her mind. Closing her eyes briefly she pushed the thought away. "What's happening?" she mumbled to herself, as she placed her hands over her face. Hope was slipping away. Inside she began to feel for the first time, that she couldn't handle him anymore.

Joshua screamed "I hate *you*! I hate your husband! And I hate this family!"

Vickie stood shocked. He had never referred to Matthew as her husband before. He had always been dad. Something she took a small amount of pride in.

An intense stare fixed onto Vickie directly from Josh, "And next time you leave," he said extremely convincingly, "I'm gonna throw the others off the balcony *with* the doll!" He then added, as he began to turn away from her, "and all of your cats too!"

Evil thoughts began racing through Joshua's mind, like his impala racing down highway 101, not knowing where they were headed, but just going fast. He stomped off to his bedroom, alone, with only his thoughts.

Vickie ran to her room too, blurting out a loud cry. Falling onto her knees and looking upward, she called out, "I don't know what to do!" She knelt, with her face in her hands, sobbing. "Heavenly Father, help me!"

Chapter Three

Threats

"I can't have Joshua threatening to throw our kids off the balcony!" Vickie exclaimed. Matthew listened to the whole story of all the events of the day. He had come in from the wood shop out in the back of the property of their home. He spent most of each day making fine wooden furniture out there for private buyers. His personally owned company provided just enough money to keep the family going. It required working long tedious days, however, Monday through Saturday, with very little time to spend in the house with the family. It seemed this had become a regular event, coming in to the turmoil of the *Joshua trials*, except now it was escalating to a new level.

"I think we need to call the police," Matthew threatened. "I won't lose my children to that unmanageable boy!" His solid stoic manner gave way to his emotions. Matthew had never spoken that way about Joshua, but his love and concern for the safety for his own children, at last, had over powered his desire to be the wonder father he had dreamed of being for Joshua.

Vickie wept. She couldn't disagree. Her heart broke while imagining her son being reported to the authorities. "How could I have let this get so out of hand?" she thought.

Matthew stood next to her, placing one arm around her shoulder, while wiping the tears from her eyes with his other hand. He looked into her eyes with sadness, shaking his head, "I've tried so hard to make this work. But..."

Vickie interrupted, "Shh... touching his lips with her index finger. It's O.K. I understand."

It was silent in the house. All of the kids were once again watching the TV in the living room, except Joshua. He had hidden himself in the hallway, out of his parents view from the kitchen and listened to their whole conversation. "The police!" he thought. He never imagined in his crazy thinking that his dad, of all people in the universe, would even consider the option. Not happy with what he was hearing, he began formulating a plan. He then walked out into the kitchen with his hands placed onto his hips, stating matter of factly, "I can take care of myself. I don't need you guys anymore!"

"Josh, uhh, what are you saying?" Vickie replied, turning toward Josh, then glancing briefly back at Matthew, very surprised by Josh's appearance in the kitchen.

"I can move out. Live on my own," Josh bluntly stated back to them both, with an empty stare in his eyes at them both. "Luck O' the Irish!" he said strangely.

Matthew jumped in stating instructively, ignoring the inappropriate saying, "You can't do that, Joshua, because you are under eighteen and not old enough to live on your own." He turned and reached for the phone on the wall.

After nine months of family counseling, required by the authorities and with Joshua promising to behave, Vickie and Matthew decided things were going well enough to make it on their own without the outside day by day guidance it had taken to manage Joshua. The counseling helped in that Vickie and Matthew began to feel validated in their concerns about Joshua. They learned some new communication techniques and realized that they needed to appear *more fair* in their handling of the other children. They both felt that the day they had called the police on Joshua was a real turning point in their lives with handling him.

Joshua had made it to his seventeenth birthday now. "Just one more year and we will be able to let him move out and things will get so much easier around here," Vickie whispered into Matthew's ear, as she sat next to him on their bed the evening after the family celebrated a small party for Joshua with just their kids and a dozen frosted chocolate cupcakes. The children had thoughtfully made birthday cards for Josh, hoping that he would be nice to them in return. Vickie bought Joshua a walkman CD player and his favorite CD, _Thriller_, by Michael Jackson. "I know it will all get better after he leaves," she continued to whisper.

Matthew sat silently, listening. If he agreed, he would be admitting that her son was the cause of much of their problems- he didn't want to go there. If he disagreed, he would be lying, and he couldn't do that either. So he sat, quietly... for the moment.

"Mom! Dad!" yelled ten year old Nathan, their usually well behaved son. "He has a knife!" he exclaimed.

Their hearts leaped out of their chests as they bolted off of their bed together. Frightened at even the thought of their child being threatened with a knife, Vickie and Matthew ran into the kitchen, pushing open their bedroom door as they ran through. They appeared before the boys in a mere moment.

Josh was holding a sharp butcher knife he had pulled out from the knife block on the counter. Josh had it aimed for Nathan, while standing across from him in a threatening stance ready to plunge it into his brother if he moved.

Young Nathan was wearing only his plaid pajama pants. He stood there with his thin and pale bare chest, feeling very vulnerable. His boy cut blonde hair was still neatly combed over to the side. He looked innocent as he was sweet in nature and genuinely frightened. Pushed up against the edge of the counter at the sink, Nathan's knees were shaking. Tears ran down his cheeks, as he sobbed in fear. "Stop him! He's gonna stab me!"

"Joshua, you put that knife down!" demanded his father.

"If that kid doesn't stop listening in on my phone calls, I'm gonna kill him!" Joshua yelled out, staring hard at Nathan with his eyes squinting a threat.

"I wasn't listening, mom, honest!" Nathan said defensively.

"You're over reacting, Josh. Now put the knife down or someone will get hurt," Vickie responded.

"You always believe *the others*, never me!" Josh complained, in a whiney tone. Still holding the knife, he snapped his attention back to Nathan, pointing the knife toward his brother's chest.

Matthew slowly walked toward Josh, staring him in the eyes, as Josh turned his sight away from Nathan, leaving the knife pointed at him, shaking. Matthew stated with a cool, controlled tone, "Hand over the knife, son. We can talk about this calmly... together."

Joshua broke down, possibly because his dad called him son. Deep down he wanted to be his real son, but he knew he wasn't. He began to cry. The knife fell from his grip onto the floor. He looked back at Nathan, with an evil stare, but he thought for a brief moment that his dad might side with him. Because of his wish to be validated, he sincerely gave his attention back to his dad. Then, the thoughts began racing through his mind again about the unfairness of his situation. Quickly his mind changed. He hated the others and all of the attention they seemed to get. He blurted out, pointing to the knife, "There, you take it! I don't need to scare the pussy boy anymore."

Matthew carefully took the knife, with a huge sigh of relief. He held it in his hand, terrified, thinking, "I can't believe this thing was pointed at my son." He snapped back to, and then he briefly tensed up again with the thought, "What if he does this again? And I'm *not* home." He looked at Joshua with a questioned expression on his face.

Then, Vickie cried out, "How can you be so cruel Joshua?" She reached over to Nathan, pulling him close to her side, interjecting her flooding emotion into the situation.

Matthew interrupted, turning his attention to her, "Honey, let's talk. Let's go into the living room and we can all talk about this together," trying to sustain the calmed emotions for the moment.

They all walked into the living room together. Matthew placed the butcher knife on top of the refrigerator as they passed it. They sat down together onto the couch, Vickie, Matthew, Nathan and Joshua. Fortunately the other kids were in bed, apparently sleeping. "Joshua, you know we cannot tolerate violent behavior in this house," began Matthew. "We have spent many months in counseling with you because we want to help you."

Josh tensed up in defense of his actions, "How would you like it if your little brothers and sisters were always spying on you and listening to all of your conversations? And, you could never have any time alone without them bugging you?"

"I understand you feel you don't have time to yourself," Matthew reiterated, trying out his new communications technique. "That is why we have given you your own room. The other children have to share their rooms. You get one to yourself so that you can have alone time."

"I'm scared you're gonna hurt your brothers and sisters," Vickie interrupted with tears pouring down her cheeks and down her neck. She couldn't hold back her feelings. "I can't trust you alone with them. Ever!" Her emotions ruled her every word. Vickie continued blurting out her deep rooted thoughts. "I wanted you to be happy with us! You never are! Nothing we ever do ever is good enough for you!" she spoke shaking her head at him.

Joshua bounced off her reaction, "I want to move out of this place. I can't stand it anymore!" Speaking with a disgusted tone in his voice, "All you ever do is blame me for everything," pointing into his chest. "Nothing your precious babies do is ever wrong!" he continued, sarcastically.

"Fine, move out," Vickie responded, grabbing a hold of Nathan's hand and squeezing it uncomfortably tight. "Where do you suppose you'll go, huh?"

"I can live out in the back," Josh said, calming his tone. He had thought about it for months, ever since the last babysitter left their house. Without fully realizing what that encompassed, Josh fantasized about the freedom he'd have away from the others, while not realizing the harshness of the life it represented. It was summertime and the weather was quite suitable for camping in their yard. The house was tucked away in a woodsy area of the town. All seemed pleasant and wonderful to a seventeen year old child. But, what would cold or wet weather do to him? Any thought past that night never entered Josh's mind. He just kept pushing his wish, "I actually *want* to live there." He said convincingly, pointing out toward the back yard.

Matthew just about interrupted, thinking the conversation was heading in the wrong direction, but pulled back his response and decided to let them work this out in their own way. He had tried his methods for all of the years he helped to raise her son, with little success. Now, he resigned himself to the extreme measures they were being driven to.

"Josh, that's crazy!" Vickie said, calming her tone with his.

"Why does it gotta be called *crazy* whenever I have an idea?" Josh kicked back at her.

"You are crazy!" Vickie exclaimed, standing to her feet. She began to escalate the situation once again, letting her emotions pour out onto Joshua. "I am sick and tired of you threatening the other kids in this house! I can't live with violence!" The memories of the violent life she experienced with Richard came flooding into her memory. She began to have difficulty separating the reality of this situation with the trauma she experienced with Richard. "I'll have you put away before you ever have the chance to hurt one of these other kids!" she continued, as she looked toward Nathan.

Nathan continued to weep as he saw his family falling apart. His heart was heavy with the worry that it was all his fault. "It's OK mom," he interjected, "Josh wasn't really gonna hurt me."

Matthew understood Nathan's intention, but couldn't let that one go. "No Nathan," he said, with a quiver in his voice. "You are not the one misbehaving here." He turned toward Joshua, "Son," he continued, "you have to realize that there are others living her as well as you. We all have to learn to live harmoniously together... somehow." He began to rub his chin with his thumb and index finger, looking downward in thought.

"There you go again, blaming me for everything!" Joshua had little tolerance left for the blaming of him for things anymore. "I'm gonna get my stuff and leave this pit you call home!" Joshua spit out. He got up and stomped all the way to his room like a two year old having a tantrum.

When he entered his room, he looked it over, thoughts racing through his mind. He grabbed an arm full of clothes, his new walkman and blankets off of his bed and headed for the kitchen, dragging half of the blanket behind him. He opened the pantry cupboard and took a handful of food and threw it in a plastic bag he found on the countertop. He looked back at Nathan and his parents, as they watched in disbelief everything he had just done. "Getting outta this place you call home!" he mumbled to them as he opened the front door and walked out of the house.

Vickie and Matthew stood stunned. Neither of them thought the evening would end as it did. Little did they know, the birthday party celebrating another year of his life that they lovingly threw for him became an ending to all of the years of his life that they had desperately tried to provide for him.

Joshua's life in that house as they had known it would never be the same.

Joshua headed out back into the wood shop and took for himself large scrap pieces of plywood. He methodically placed them into the form of a square shaped room under a large oak tree along the hillside of the back yard. He placed his blankets onto the floor of his room and draped his clothes up over the tops of the plywood walls. He lay down on his back looking up at the dark star scattered sky. The stars seemed to woo him, as if to take him home. Then, he caught the drift of cow manure in the air, as the edge of a cow pasture butted up against their back fence. Somehow, it made the moment sweeter. It fit. He turned to his side and could see the balcony of the house, two stories up, where he no longer lived. "Glad to be outta there," he mumbled to himself as he reached over for his walkman, placing the miniature sized headphones over his ears and cranked up _Beat It_.

CHAPTER FOUR

The Fort

Several months had now passed. Joshua continued to live outdoors. His *fort,* as he put it, became his home. Though Vickie didn't feel good about her own son living outside of the comfort of a home, especially now in the cold and wet of winter, she did feel safer. Inside their home she knew Joshua couldn't harm the other children and at the same time she knew, for the most part, where Josh was. She knew he was alive. She chose to believe he was most likely out of trouble and every night before she went to bed, she looked out over the balcony, to reassure herself that he was indeed there. She could see Josh faintly under the edges of the torn sheet he hung over a two by four which crossed the front side between two branches.

Vickie and Matthew had explained to the other children that the reason Josh was now living outdoors was because Joshua wanted to have his own room and he liked it outside. The other children were afraid of Josh and accepted any explanation that sounded remotely possible. Matthew changed the locks on the house, however, when Josh moved out. He always kept the doors locked- even when they were home and kept a close eye on Josh from his shop whenever he approached the house.

Joshua, dirty, smelling of rancid body odor and filthy clothing, knocked on the front door, "Open, it's me," he called out in a cracked voice. His little boy voice still popped up awkwardly at times when he was speaking in his slightly lowered, maturing voice. Asking for food once a day, Josh came to the house waiting at the door for a handout. Vickie had prepared just enough for him to eat each time. She often left gallons of water on the front porch and a case of soda every week. Her heart broke when she saw him hungry and smelly and especially when she faced him each time while locked out of the house.

Joshua stood patiently waiting for his food when his mom opened the door. He had accepted his fate, convincing himself that it was better to be on his own outside than it would be inside with *the others*. Vickie cracked open the door just enough to slip her arm out holding a paper plate loaded with a hearty beef and cheddar cheese sandwich on a sourdough roll, a pile of potato chips and two homemade chocolate chip cookies. She avoided eye contact. She held back her words. Josh grabbed the plate with both hands as Vickie released it from her grip. Josh didn't say anything. He just took the plate and turned his back to her as he carefully held his food, walking toward his fort. Vickie watched him through the crack in the doorway; a tear fell onto her cheek as she slowly closed the door. Matthew stood just outside the shop, watching the whole interaction and then stepped back inside where he was working.

Aside from acquiring his meal, Joshua found much to do every day. He took walks out of their part of the woods, strolling down a long windy road tucked into the valley into the city of Santa Rosa. He began to meet other people who lived outdoors. He had never before realized there were so many people like himself. He learned their names and befriended many of them.

It had somehow turned springtime. It seemed winter finished one day and spring started the next with blue skies and warm air. Joshua decided to take a walk and explore a different part of the city where there was an old stone, moss covered bridge. He sat down just underneath in a shady spot to cool off. He threw his backpack onto the ground and opened it up to get out the sandwich that his mother had prepared for him. Suddenly a very skinny weathered old man came up from behind him, snatching it out of his hand. "Hey, that's mine," Josh cried out. The hunched over, toothless old man simply began to stuff the sandwich into his mouth while walking away. Josh wasn't happy; he knew his next meal wasn't until the next day, so he set out back to town where he knew there was a grocery store. He had been to that Safeway store before, but didn't always find food in its dumpster. He walked toward the dumpster this time hoping there'd be something for him to eat inside. "Score!" Josh called out, as he reached in and pulled out an entire box of Frosted Flakes. The box was dented, but entirely sealed. He tore open the top as he began stuffing handfuls of the whitened flakes into his mouth.

Josh quickly learned that there were also people out there who would do anything to get food, and soon became careful to hide all of the food he had been given from his mom and any food he scored from a dumpster dive.

Josh became lonely. That afternoon a young twenty three year old homeless man nick named Scowl bumped into him, shortly after the successful dumpster dive. Josh invited him over to his fort. Josh had met Scowl several times downtown in Santa Rosa. He seemed to have a lot in common with Josh. Scowl's parents had kicked him out of his house and he too hated his brother. The both of them wound up hanging around dumpsters for food and walked the streets together looking at the people passing, as if it were a sport. They didn't talk much, but they laughed a lot about things they both seemed to think were funny.

Scowl had a problem with looking at pornography. It seemed like it took up a large amount of his day. He carried magazines in his back pocket wherever he went. As they walked to Josh's fort, Scowl pulled out a Playboy for Josh to look at. "Check it out!" he said, as he opened the centerfold, slowly stroking the picture from top to bottom with two fingers.

"Sick!" Josh replied. He smiled as he too began to check out the centerfold. "Where'd you get it?" he asked.

"Picked it up at the park," he said with a smirk. "They're everywhere. You can get 'em at any Seven Eleven."

"Sweet," Josh said, with his eyes wide open. He had never seen any pornography before.

Scowl had a reputation of scaring off women with his scowling looks; that was where he had picked up his nickname. He had resorted to pictures to satisfy his sexual appetite. He was always unshaven, and had black curly frizzed out hair. His lips were full and his skin very tan. He wore baggy worn out blue jeans and an oversized tee shirt. If he had been cleaned up, he would have been a good looking young man.

The introduction of pornography opened up a new world for Joshua. He began hanging the nude foldouts from every magazine he could buy or steal up onto his plywood walls, covering every inch of the space. Every week or so, Scowl would drop by to visit. They didn't talk much, but stared for hours at the nude pictures.

Another friend of Josh's also began to come by often to visit. He was real trouble. He sold and stole drugs. His nickname was Narko. He was a little psycho at times.

Joshua only smoked pot with him at first. It seemed to make Josh feel better about his life and his troubles didn't seem so bad. Narko worked at making friends with Josh, telling him he was cool and a lot of fun to hang out with. Josh had been so lonely that it felt good to have a friend.

Narko was thirty one; he had been homeless off and on for years. His ability to manipulate a conversation sucked Josh right into his lifestyle of drug abuse. He had most of his teeth missing, but in spite of his hideous smile and obvious lack of sincerity, he managed to make friends.

While hanging out with Josh, Narko had often noticed the mushrooms growing in the cow pasture behind Josh's house. "What do ya think about them shrooms out back there," he said while pointing to the cow pasture. "Think they're any good?"

Josh's hadn't noticed the mushrooms before and didn't know of their significance. "I don't know," he answered shrugging his shoulders. The pot smoking was enough for him at the time and Josh didn't know much about any other drugs that were out there.

Narko got up and walked over to the cow pasture. He hopped the fence and began collecting the mushrooms. He took off his shirt and made a makeshift sack out of it, filling it with the shrooms.

Josh watched with curiosity, wondering, "what the hell's he doin'?" Joshua never cared much for how mushrooms tasted as food, but was willing to try anything. He simply continued to sit, watching Narko break them off at the stump one at a time.

"These here are *magic mushrooms*," Narko said, holding one between his fingertips after he returned with a sack full. "We'll let them dry out in the back here behind your fort." He emptied the shirt of the mushrooms and spread them out to dry on a piece of ply wood that was lying there in the dirt. "Think they'll be OK sittin' there Josh?"

"Sure," he said with no worries, as the family usually avoided him as much as possible.

"Well, I'm gonna take a few with me, if that's OK with you. Think I'll give 'em a try." Narko picked up his shirt and began putting it back on. He stuffed a couple of the mushrooms into a pocket in the front and left the fort.

Soon, this became their favorite drug of all. Narko came over just about every day.

"Check this out," Narko said, while spinning in a circle in the field behind the fort.

"What a ya doin?" Josh said, watching him spin around like a kid, then land on his butt.

"Just playin," Narko answered, with his toothless smile.

Josh's face was numb. He began yawning. Then, he thought he heard a baby crying from behind him, but when he turned to see it, it was not there.

"Seein things?" Narko said. "Pretty funny, huh?"

""Creepy, actually," Josh mumbled back, as his words came out slower than usual.

At that moment Josh saw a leprechaun literally jump out in front of him. The leprechaun called out to Joshua, "Lock O' the Irish!

Startled, Josh stepped back so fast he too fell onto his butt. "Shit, did you see that?"

"What, kid?" Narko replied, preoccupied with his own trip.

"A damn green leprechaun just jumped out in front of me!"

Narko just laughed.

Soon many of his new friends came over just to get some mushrooms. The two of them sold whatever they could and ate the rest. Joshua ate his shrooms whenever as often as he wanted.

About once a week, the oldest of Josh's siblings, Kirstey, would come out and bring her brother a sandwich that she had made because of the compassion she had for his situation. She was a quiet young teen, intelligent and very well behaved. Her silky long brunette hair was always pulled neatly into a ponytail. She wore homemade dresses her mother had sewn, giving her a country girl look. Her pure blue eyes always seem to look into a person, as though she could read their minds.

When Kirstey came out to give him his sandwich each time, Josh would make sure to meet her far enough away so she couldn't see inside the fort. "She don't need to see these," he told himself. He looked at his pictures. His sense of conscience was still intact.

This day, with a tuna sandwich in hand, Kirstey walked toward the fort. As she approached his fort, she smelled an odd odor. She didn't know it was the smell of marijuana. As she breathed it in, she thought, "What's that awful smell!" She continued walking, convincing herself that it must have come from the cow pasture out back. Josh took a last hit of the joint when he noticed her coming with his lunch, and quickly put it out. He placed it behind a rock inside his fort, where he kept things hidden from everyone. He had eaten a mushroom a couple of hours prior, and then smoked a joint. He felt pretty high, so he decided this time to hide himself from Kirstey.

When Kirstey got to the fort, she didn't see Josh inside. It was unusual for Josh to be gone since he looked forward to the sandwich each time she came out with it. When she looked inside, she saw the nude pictures hanging in an unorganized fashion all over the inside like wall paper, something she hadn't ever seen before. It scared her and she quickly turned away. She decided to look around the back of his fort where the huge old gnarled tree trunk came up from the ground and still didn't see him. She walked back to the entrance and knelt at the floor, trying not to look inside again, placing the sandwich down onto the floor. Just then, Josh jumped out from behind a pile of wood he had gathered from the shop and yelled, "Boo!" with his hands at both sides of his face and fingers spread wide open.

Kirstey jumped up. Her heart leaped. Then she smiled after gasping a breath and said, "Josh you scared me!"

"The world is a scary place little sister," he said eerily. "There are people and things everywhere. Even when you think they aren't there. Wham!" he slapped his hands together, while jumping up, "Boom! They pop up in front of you!"

Kirstey felt nervous about Josh's behavior. She couldn't understand what he meant. She noticed his eyes were dilated, making his pupils very large. He looked different, thinner, and his face was broken out with bad acne. His body was filthy and he stank. He seemed hyper and talked strangely. She quietly backed away from him, walking slowly backwards, twirling her ponytail hair between her fingers, and not saying a word. When she felt safe enough, she turned around and ran away from the fort back to the house. She hid the experience in her heart, as she felt guilty about her brother having to live outside all of this time in his little fort, while she lived comfortably inside.

CHAPTER FIVE

Moving On

"WHAT ARE WE GONNA GET him? He can't even take care of the things he already has," Vickie said to Matthew, while discussing Joshua's upcoming eighteenth birthday. The two of them were in their bathroom finishing their showers and getting ready for the day. It was early May and the weather was beautiful outside, with the trees and flowers blooming and the smell of lilacs in the air. It felt like the springtime had brought a newness into their lives, with the prospect of Joshua being of age and able to move out on his own.

"I hadn't thought about that quite yet." Matthew began to ponder the thought. He considered Joshua's behavior, as he had lived, now, for a year outdoors. He had been keeping out of their way with the exception of only a couple occurrences where he made threatening statements to his children. These were minor and

Joshua seemed too preoccupied with his own life to get involved with theirs. "Ya know, aside from getting him his birthday gift, we also ought to let him know we are moving," he said with hesitation. "But... I am not sure we should tell him where," Matthew quickly added, as he begun to brush his large white, fairly straight teeth. He had a smile that could stand out in a crowd of people.

"I don't want him to know. As a matter of fact, I think we should buy him a ticket to his *father's* house for his birthday present," Vickie retorted. "Then he would be even farther away from us when we move to Colorado." Vickie had been thinking about this for quite awhile. Though she felt sad about her feelings toward her son, she knew it was time to let him go.

Even though Joshua's natural father had had nothing to do with his upbringing after the age of two, he still genetically contributed to the person Josh became, a difficult and unruly child... now young adult. Richard's mother, Josh's grandma Mitchem, had kept contact with them throughout his entire childhood, always caring for him as her only grandson. Vickie struggled with the conflict she felt within. She never doubted her love for her son, but whenever Josh misbehaved she couldn't help but see Richard's face, actions, and most of all his eyes. Richard's eyes were evil in her opinion. They seemed to stare past her, never connecting with her. Josh had the same stare. She'd never had that with her other children. They had their father's nature, for the most part, sweet and gentle. Vickie needed a break and she couldn't ignore the fact that Josh was very much different from her other children.

"Are you suggesting we move half way across the country without even telling him?" Matthew didn't feel good about that idea, it just seemed wrong. Shaking his head, he walked into his closet. He reached for his Jovan Musk which always sat on the same spot on the shelf in his side of the closet, and sprayed the smallest amount under each armpit and on his chest. He pulled a shirt from the rack and began to put it on.

"Honey, I love my son, but the constant threat he poses to the other children is very disconcerting, to say the least," Vickie said with a mouthful of toothpaste and her toothbrush scrubbing her teeth. She spit out the toothpaste, "I just think he can live with his father for awhile and, who knows, maybe Richard has changed. Maybe he'll be good for him," she tried to convince herself. She rinsed out her mouth and joined Matthew in the closet.

"Wow!" Matthew quickly responded. "I never thought I'd hear you say that!" He stood back from her in amazement, then stepped up to her, kissing her briefly on her cheek, as if to say he agreed with her.

"Seriously, honey," Vickie said, with a slight smile, enjoying the small intimate moment she just had with her husband. "Richard's mother has always cared about Josh, buying him birthday and Christmas gifts, and I know she would love to see him too. She could be there for Josh while Richard has him. I know they must still live close by each other."

"I see your point. Are you certain you are making a good decision for Joshua?"

"Matthew," she responded, "Josh has asked hundreds, well maybe not hundreds, but many times to go live with his dad. Maybe those weren't just idol threats. Maybe he really does want to."

"O.K.," he responded, giving her a pat on her butt. "Let's get him a bus ticket," he said with a little chuckle. "Let's arrange it to happen just after his birthday."

"Phew!" Vickie massaged her temple a moment. "I will get the ticket and, I think he'll need a suitcase too. We might as well do both." She followed Matthew out of their closet and back out of the bathroom and into their bedroom. "O.K?" Matthew nodded in agreement. Though her husband was supportive of their decision, it was still stressful for Vickie to think about doing such a thing, especially now, because it meant making contact with Richard.

"Hello?" Vickie answered the portable phone while carrying a load of laundry loosely in her arms. She walked to the couch in her new living room and plopped the pile down onto it. As the clothes fell, she caught a whiff of the fresh Tide laundry soap she had used for many years especially for the fragrance it left in the clothing. Fluffy, her white Persian, jumped up onto the couch, snuggling next to the clothes. She smiled briefly, and then listened to the person on the other end of the line.

"Is this the mother of Joshua Mitchem?" the voice asked with a quick delivery.

"Yes," it caught her by surprise. She hadn't thought of that name for a long time. Even when Josh was living with them, she rarely thought of his actual last name, always thinking of him as a Peterson. "Who is this?" she began to wonder.

"Hi, Ms. Mitchem," the voice continued.

"Uh, I'm his mother, but my last name is Peterson," she quickly interjected.

"Oh, I apologize," he continued. "Uh, your son has requested we contact you. He has given us your number. We have him on hold in the Santa Rosa jail here in California. We have some concerns about him we'd like to discuss with you."

The information was coming so quickly, Vickie could hardly catch up with them in her mind. "In jail? What for?"

"He's been arrested for Grand Theft Auto." The man on the other end of the line didn't skip a beat and continued, "We'll need your address so we can send you some paperwork to fill out and sign." The man's voice continued in a matter of fact tone. "Uh, my name is Officer Sutton," as if realizing he didn't introduce himself, "I am handling his case."

"Case?" Vickie tried to catch up with what the officer was saying, then asked, "If he has been arrested, doesn't he just have to serve his time and..."

The officer interrupted her, "Yes. That is true, but at this time he is sitting in his jail cell speaking gibberish of some sort. We cannot understand what he is saying. It sounds like he's speaking German," the officer began, slowing his delivery, "but one of the other officers here speaks a little German and says it isn't German at all. Does your son speak another language that you know of, Ms. Uhh... Peterson?" He asked the question in a disingenuous tone, it was obvious to Vickie he knew it wasn't a real language.

"No, he doesn't," Vickie quickly snapped back.

"We're going to have him evaluated by a psychiatrist," the officer continued. "We were able to obtain a written consent from your son at one point to discuss his situation with you. I expect this is alright with you as well."

"Yes, certainly," Vickie consented, "can you please send me a copy of what the uh, psychiatrist says?"

"Yes, let me get your address," Officer Sutton stated. "I understand you once lived in this area. Did you recently move? I don't recognize your area code," he stated while slowing his words. "Where are you now?" he continued as he reread the phone number he just dialed.

"Pueblo, Colorado. It's been a year, but we're still settling in. It's been quite a change for us. Uh, a good one, that is."

When the Peterson family had moved from California, they'd rented a large Ryder moving truck and packed up their 1987 maroon colored Chevy Van, hauling the furniture, the clothing and all of their belongings along with all of their children, except, of course, Joshua.

"Good. So, what's the address?" the officer asked. He proceeded to gather the information he needed and then ended the conversation with, "I'll be in contact with you soon. Thank you for your cooperation."

When the paperwork arrived, a week later, Vickie quickly opened it up. All week long she'd worried about the crime her son had committed. She was mortified to think *her* own flesh and blood could have been arrested. She was so embarrassed about the whole thing that it took her several days to even discuss it with Matthew. "I don't dare tell any of my new friends at my church," she quietly whispered, "they'll surely think I'm a bad mother." Her hands shook nervously as she ripped open the top of the envelope.

"Schizophrenia?" she said slowly and quietly with her eyebrows pulled together tightly. She began to read the psychiatrist's report, which showed up first in the stack of papers she pulled out… "Paranoid? Too!" she read. "This guy's got to be a quack." She mumbled softly to herself. "Joshua's disobedient, for sure, but crazy? I don't think so!" She paused for a moment, remembering actually calling him crazy, but quickly shook the thought from her mind. She recalled just then, the officer on the phone saying Joshua had been speaking gibberish. Nothing like that ever happened before with Josh. "Maybe he's on something. That's it. I'm sure," she convinced herself. She was so involved with the psychiatrist's report that she couldn't move past it to the charges brought against her son that were written on the remainder of the pages she held tightly in her hands.

With all new friends in their new found community, the Peterson's felt they had begun a new life there. Their children were involved in the community, playing in the band, each taking up a variety instruments. They settled into their schools and for the first time in their lives, were able to bring home school and church friends without worrying about Joshua being home to scare them off.

Kirstey had written Joshua's grandma inquiring about her brother shortly after they had moved to Colorado, but was surprised by Josh's grandma Mitchem's response. Grandma Mitchem had written back almost immediately, stating "Joshua came to visit, sure enough," she began, "I was so thrilled to see him at the bus station that day." She continued, "But the visit was awfully short. I hadn't seen him for all of those years and I sure did want to spend some time with him. Just a few days after he had arrived, though, he got right back on that bus." She explained that she thought his dad had bought him the ticket. Kirstey, along with the rest of the family at that time, assumed Josh had found himself a place to live somewhere and chose to keep his distance. They had moved several states from him, pretty much admitting their strong desire to be away from him. The family knew, though, that if Josh really wanted to contact them that he could get their number from his grandma Mitchem.

"I'm not sure I know what this means," Vickie said to Matthew, as she walked toward him in the kitchen with her eyes staring at the page in front of her. The kitchen was a lot smaller than their old one, but this house they owned. It had come with a well used, kind of built in, cooking smell. It was a small contributing factor they noticed, when deciding to buy the home making it immediately feel like home. They were first time homeowners and were learning the joys and difficulties of having their own home. "I don't get it. It looks like they'll most likely be sending him to a psychiatric institution after the arraignment" Vickie said as her voice started to drop to a low tone. "It says he wasn't found to be, uh, mentally competent." She read further, "Atascadero Mental Hospital? That's where he will spend criminal time?"

Matthew stood frozen in the kitchen, staring at her as she walked toward him. His mouth began to slip open as his thoughts began to wrap around the idea of Joshua getting locked up for being *mentally incompetent*. "You know he's a good liar. He's so good he's got them all fooled!" he retorted.

"Apparently," she continued to read, "He was found in the front seat of a dump truck of all things. They found him in it parked in a Safeway parking lot," she said with shocky tone in her voice, "in the middle of the night!"

"That doesn't make him crazy," Matthew insisted, "A criminal, yes!" he paused, "but crazy? I don't think so!"

Chapter six

Luck o' the Irish!

I COULDN'T BELIEVE MY EYES! With my front door swung wide open, I stood just inside the doorway, shocked! I then slowly eased the door closing it behind me, realizing who I was looking at. About six foot tall and slightly hunched over, the shaggily dressed, scruffy and sparsely bearded young man looked me over and said, "Hi Aunt Sherry." With his high pitched halfway deepened voice he sort of giggled and asked, "Is Sean and Pat here?" When he smiled through his dry cracked lips, I could see that his yellow colored teeth were filled with food chunks and hadn't been brushed for quite a long time. His light brown hair was long and straggly. It had separated clumps stuck together with grease, hanging half way into his face. The rest tucked behind his ears.

The young man in front of me was little Joshy, except he wasn't so little anymore. I was stunned. "This couldn't be Joshy," I thought, "here all the way from the bay area in California to Reno." I began to wonder how he knew where we lived.

My husband, a computer engineer, got transferred to Reno from the bay area with the company he worked for and I reluctantly moved with him. We had four children who were becoming teenagers at the time and I feared what the influences of the open life style there would do to them. I hated the city from the start. Because of my strong Christian values, the lifestyle there seemed contrary to the life style I had imagined raising children in. But I always prayed for protection there, and believed God would keep us safe. I worked full time as an operating room nurse. Though I desired to be home more because my children needed me there, I was persuaded by my husband to work full time. The trials were long and hard, but we managed to get through them. We provided well for our family and there were a lot of fun times spent vacationing and enjoying life.

Joshua's black tee shirt was so dirty I could hardly make out the picture of some punk rock band on the front. The shirt was torn along the hem, hanging down just past his jean pockets. I could see the black outline of flames tattooed onto his upper right arm just above his elbow. His blue jeans were loose, sagging down just under his butt with his boxer shorts showing around the upper edge just enough to cover his bottom. A black leather studded belt strapped around his hips snugged them into position. He wore tennis shoes which were so worn the soles were separated half way from each shoe and the laces were up about three holes and then tied closed with brown and frayed ends into little knots. He looked filthy dirty; I hesitated in inviting him into the house, thinking he might have been carrying lice.

"Uh, Joshua, come in," I said, feeling obligated, as I opened the door further. It was cool outside in the early part of fall. I had on a pair of comfortable black jean shorts and a green V necked tee shirt. I felt the cool air coming in and was then motivated to get the door shut. I motioned for him to come in.

"Thanks," he said as he stepped in through the doorway.

I almost gagged, as he moved passed me. I breathed in the most disgusting odor. It was more than the dirty clothes smell I had smelled before on my own boys when they wore a sweaty shirt more than a day in a row. His extreme halitosis I only remembered smelling once from an old man I once met who had black rotting teeth! "What am I doing, letting this person, though he may be my nephew, into my house?" I thought to myself. As Josh brushed by me, his shirt barely touched the skin on my arm. A chill shivered down my spine. I remember a creepy feeling coming over me. Goose bumps popped up on my arms. I immediately lightly rubbed over them with my hand, almost as if rubbing away his contact from me.

Just then Sean came down the stairs and into the living room, "Dude, Josh is that you?" he asked, while looking him over with a smile. The smile quickly turned into a serious look. Sean was just a month older than Josh, and they had been the closest of the cousins while growing up. He dressed similarly to Josh and was about the same size, except he was clean. Sean stopped a few feet from Josh.

"Yea," Josh smiled in return.

"Whoa, what's that smell?" He stepped back a moment, then continued walking toward him. Sean realized the smell was coming from Josh. "Dude, you need some clean clothes? I got some you can wear."

Josh half smiled, "O.K." while shrugging his shoulders. Sean showed him up the stairs and into his bedroom where he gave Josh a clean pair of jeans and a fresh tee shirt to wear.

As they were heading up to Sean's room, I began to remember how Sean and Josh had spent much of their days away from school together when we lived in Petaluma California. I always called him Joshy when he was little, just as I called Sean "Seany" I think it was a mom thing. My sister and I had gotten together about once a month, especially in the warmer times of the year, for about seven years while they were in grade school. The boys then had fun playing outdoors, camping, hiking and swimming. Our family gatherings were centered around the kids, always finding places to go that they could run and play.

"What's going on?" my husband, Kim, asked as he came into the house from the garage. He had heard the commotion inside and decided to check out the situation. Kim could be hot tempered when pushed. He was a classic full blooded Irish man in personality. Raised with seven brothers, he had learned to fight at a young age. "Who were you talking to?" he asked, while stepping toward us, with the look of a fighter ready to go "a round."

I knew we were in for some trouble, "Uh, Joshy's here," I began.

"It stinks down here! What the hell's going on?" Kim began looking around suspiciously.

"Sean just came down and saw Joshy here. He just went back up to his room, and..."

Kim interrupted, "Why does it smell like rotten shit?" He turned back to the staircase, with his face turning as red as what was left of the red hair on his head and began climbing the stairs back up to Sean's room.

When he got to the top of the stairs, he quickly stepped in front of Sean's closed door and began knocking loudly. "Sean, open the door!" he demanded.

"Whoa, dad, chill out," Sean said as he opened the door, looking his father in the eyes.

Kim walked into the messy room, pushing Sean aside. Clothes were thrown everywhere, but it was easy to spot the clothes that Josh had been wearing. They were on top of a pile, stinky and filthy. "Give em to me," he said, putting out his hand.

Sean grabbed them and tossed them to his dad. "Here, take 'em," he said without hesitation.

Kim caught the soiled clothing, holding them away from his body. Josh was sitting on Sean's bed, watching, but not saying a word. "Josh, go take a shower!" He commanded. He then pointed Joshua towards the bathroom, and turned back to the stairs, quickly going down and around the corner straight to the laundry room. He plopped down the shirt, pants, and the crusty looking, worn out socks onto the washer. He began feeling the pants pockets, as he would any pair of pants going into the wash, and discovered a lump in one of them. He gingerly put his index and middle fingers into the pocket, taking hold of a baggie half filled with yellow rocks. Kim's heart skipped a beat, as he realized he was most likely holding crack or some kind of illegal drug. So he quickly walked over to the bathroom which was next to the laundry room, and without another thought about it, instinctively threw the baggy into the toilet and flushed it down.

I listened to the whole exchange between Kim and the boys from downstairs. I had gone into the kitchen; I think to use up my nervous energy by cooking dinner. When I heard the toilet flush, I left the kitchen and asked Kim, "What are you doing?"

"Do you know what I just found?" he asked angrily.

I didn't really want to know, because whenever Kim was this mad I could never seem to say the right thing. "What did you find?"

"Yellow rocks in a baggie! What do you suppose that could be?" he asked sarcastically.

Kim made me feel like I had committed the crime. "Is that what you just flushed," not getting to finish as Kim interrupted.

"Yes! Why'd you let this creep into our house?" he demanded.

"He's our nephew," I said, kind of confused about the situation.

"He's our nephew," he mocked me; "He's a drug addict!" he then clarified. "I want him out of here by tomorrow!" Kim commanded. He knew Josh was away from home and would most likely need to spend the night. His tone softened, "I'll buy him a bus ticket to his parent's house if I have to."

"O.K." I said obediently. "I'll let the boys know he can't stay."

Pat walked into the house. "Hey mom," he said while heading for the kitchen.

"Hi Pat," I said, holding back my voice.

"What's wrong?" Pat asked. Pat had a big heart, but he too pushed the limits in our family. He knew me well enough to see that I was holding back emotionally. This time it didn't involve anything he had done.

"Oh, nothing, really," I said, struggling to pull my thoughts together. "Uh, Joshy's here."

"Josh? Cousin Josh?" he said back curiously. "Where is he?"

"Upstairs taking a shower," I answered.

"Whoa! Dude, a shower?" he said, questioning the strangeness of that happening. Pat was street wise and could smell a rat from a mile away. He knew something was up.

"Uh, yeah," I said, "He was pretty filthy dirty. I think you and Sean ought to take him out for awhile this evening and, uh, well hangout. I think he could use some friends."

"Sure, that'd be fun," Pat said back to me. Pat liked the idea of getting to go out, but intuitively knew there would be trouble.

It had been several years since we had seen Joshua. My sister had kept in touch with us since we moved from California to Reno, but we all were so busy with our families, that it was hard to keep up with the details of each other's lives. We did know about Josh being sent to his natural father's house for his eighteenth birthday, a story the whole family heard about, but didn't know about his arrest when he went back to Santa Rosa to live. It had been a year since the arrest, I later learned. Now Josh seemed ready to reconnect with his family.

The next day after Josh's arrival to our home, Kim had Josh change back into the clean clothes that he had washed for him. "At least they are clean now," he said when he handed them back to Josh. He didn't waste any time getting Josh to the bus station where he bought him a ticket to Pueblo, Colorado. He made sure Josh boarded the bus waiting as he gladly waived him good bye!

"Mom, did you hear what happened yesterday after we left the house with Josh?" Sean asked, just after his dad left the house with Josh for the bus station.

"No. What happened?" I asked, as I plopped down onto the couch to rest. The whole Joshua visit had made me feel exhausted. I put my feet up onto the oval shaped glass topped coffee table. "How does Vickie do it," I thought.

"Whoa, it was weird, dude. Man, we all went for a ride in my car," he began. "You know my friends, they're all pretty cool with things," he continued. Sean was always considered one of the cool kids among his friends. He had a crazy sense of humor that could get a depressed person laughing at the smallest things and so he made friends with just about everybody. "Well, we were driving down Virginia Street. We thought we'd show Josh downtown." Sean began to pace in front of me, recalling the event.

"Who all was with you?" I asked.

"Pat, Ryan and Chris," he quickly answered, excited to tell the rest of his story. "We were all talking, ya know, just about regular stuff. Then, Josh told us why he was arrested in Santa Rosa."

"He did?" I quickly responded, wondering myself what he had done.

"Yeah, it's kinda funny, actually," he said with a smile on one side of his mouth. "So, like he said he found this dump truck filled with dirt in the dump bed."

"Dump truck?" I questioned.

"Yeah, it gets better... uh, so he said he saw the keys left in the ignition, so he thought *they didn't want it anymore,*" he dragged out the words, emphasizing Josh's thinking. Sean's face lit up as it always did when he told a good story with his eyebrows raised and his voice going higher. We all started asking him about it. Pat asked him where he went with it. You know Pat, always trying to figure out *why.* Anyway," Sean couldn't be more into the story, "Josh said he drove it all around Santa Rosa, looking for a place *to dump the dirt out for them.*" Sean let out a laugh, then continued, "We all laughed." He shook his head, looking down for a moment, recalling the moment. "Can you believe it? He thought he was helping them!" He continued, "Anyway, Chris asked how he got caught."

Yeah, I was wondering about that too," I added.

"Well, Mom, he said he *had to park it somewhere where he couldn't get caught,*" Sean was loving this, dragging out every word to his favorite portion of the story, "*so he parked it in the Safe-way parking lot!*" Sean busted out laughing. "Like, it would be *safe there!*"

I couldn't help but laugh a little. I asked Sean, "So did he tell you how he got caught?"

"Yeah, so it was like midnight and he was sleeping in the front seat, still *in the parking lot,*" he continued taking short breaths in, pressing into the story, "and a cop came banging on the window, he said. Then, Josh said the cop told him the truck was reported stolen and wanted to know why he took it!" Sean kept going, "so get this, Josh told the cop that he thought the owner didn't want it cuz they *left their keys inside!* And then," Sean continued with a laugh, "Josh told the cop that he did them a favor by dumping their dirt for them and wondered *why they were so upset about it.*"

"Wow, that's strange. I feel for Vickie," I said quietly to myself.

"What'd you say?" Sean questioned.

"Nothing, go on," I mumbled.

"But then it got weird," Sean continued, "Josh started mumbling." Sean paused, while he thought for a moment. "Then we stopped talking and heard him speaking like to another person... except there was no one there where he was looking. You couldn't even understand what he was saying! It was funny at first," Sean continued, "We were joking with him and laughing." Sean paused, "Then, Mom, it was straight up weird." Sean looked down, his genuine care for friends and family caused him to stop and think about his feelings for his cousin. With a serious tone in his voice, he continued, "And then, Josh started bragging about killing some bum under the Golden Gate Bridge when he was in San Francisco. Everyone got quiet," he said, trying to believe it was probably a lie. "We got this freaky feeling, even Pat and Chris felt it," he said to me, "like it was supernatural."

"What do you mean, exactly?" I asked, wondering what else more could possibly be going on with little Joshy.

"Seriously, mom, he was saying like weird words. Like seriously, like he was having a conversation with someone. Like we weren't even there to him," he said, shaking his head. "Then my friends started asking me who he was and where he came from. They were asking me all kinds of questions about him. I didn't know what to say," he said biting his lip while thinking. "Then, I got embarrassed to admit he was even related to me!" he said with a nervous laugh.

"Wow, this is all so scary, what ended up happening?" I asked.

Sean answered, "Pat kept asking who he was talking to and what bum. Pat kept talking to him, trying to figure out what he was talking about, while the rest of us were in shock."

"Sounds like he's schizophrenic," I interjected. "It sure looked like it from what I had seen and now what you are telling me." I began to put it together, "I had seen quite a few schizophrenic patients when I was in nursing school, doing my psychology rotation. I never imagined my own nephew would be one, though." I thought about the many childhood years when he played with "the cousins" and he seemed like a regular kid. Yeah, he had his problems, but all kids did.

"Like he's crazy?" Sean asked.

"Well, it's a mental disorder." I said instructively, trying to be sensitive to the situation and fully realizing the impact it must be having on my sister as well. "They hear voices and often see things, like people. They hallucinate," I explained.

"Oh, totally. That's what he was doing. Man, it was weird. He even freaked *me* out." Sean said, chuckling to himself. "I can't believe we used to hang out together. He was pretty normal then. He-" Sean paused, remembering back to a boating vacation we had once where we took Josh skiing, dropping him, Josh and Pat off on a small island in the center of the lake. Sean had told stories about Joshua pulling his pants down and mooning the boats passing by and talking about things that were way out. Sean questioned Josh's behavior then. "He, uh, well Mom, ya know, did some dumb stuff when we took him out boating before." He was on a roll, "I remember him calling out to the boaters with his pants pulled all of the way down, 'Luck O' the Irish!' I thought he was jealous of us at the time," Josh recalled. "And remember what he did to their cat? I can't believe it survived the fall from the balcony. Oh yeah, and the time," he stopped. Sean looked at me and then realized I wasn't taking too much interest in recalling the bad things of the past. I never did.

"So dad took him to the bus station?" he said as he uncomfortably changed the subject.

"Yeah," I responded. "He didn't want him around here at all. I can't say I blame him, either."

CHAPTER SEVEN

GRAND PARENTING

"LOOK IT'S THE MCCALL'S," THE proud grandparents called out as we pulled into their driveway and the kids began running out of the car. Seany was the first to run up and give his grandma a big hug. Just as quickly as he left her arms, he was in his grandpa's embrace. The other kids followed suit. This was one of the happiest moments of their young lives, visiting grandma and grandpa out in the country where they could run and play all day long.

I remember the day well. Long before the kids became teenagers. All of the cousins played together so well.

Soon the other cars started pulling up to the house, one after another, filled with cousins. There were lots of kids to play with, twenty three in all. The last carload to arrive was the Peterson family. As the little ones began to climb out of their seats in the car, Joshy trampled over them throwing open the car door and running up to the house.

By now all 3500 sq. ft. of the house was full. Easter day was in full action, a tradition the family looked forward to every year. I recall Joshy and Seany and a couple of the other boy cousins about their age running off into the open grass fields out in back of the huge house that separated the scattered homes in this community settled around Lake Comanche, California.

The warm weather, fully blue sky and beautiful green grass accented with wild flowers, made for a dream like land for the kids to play in. While my mother, my sisters and I prepared the food for lunch and dinner, talking about everything from Camden's first tooth to mom's latest doctor's appointment, the guys hung out in the living room listening to repeated story after story about my dad's work life before retiring. My father always came out a hero in every story. I had heard them so many times that I could mentally tell the stories with him.

Just before lunch, my dad, an intelligent six foot three inch, bold, yet loving man, called the kids in from the four corners of the earth. He placed his two index fingers into his mouth, and then taking in a brisk firm breath blew hard. The whistle travelled for miles, I am sure of it. The pierce sound caused our ears to ring afterword in the kitchen. He followed with, "Time to eat!" He stood tall, with his large gut hanging over his belt, hands on his hips, and a half smile, while watching the kids begin to pour into the house.

The youngest of the kids came running from the upstairs first, in a single line down the spiral staircase.

Their little legs could hardly go as fast as they meant for them to. Whatever little toys they were in the middle of playing with in the oversized play room upstairs, they clutched tightly in their hands as they struggled to hold onto the staircase railing. Then the front and back doors opened, almost as if on cue together, the boys running in from the back and the girls from the front. The girls had flowers in hand that they'd gathered from a large mound my mom maintained in front filled with imported flowers of all sorts. The beautiful flowers blossomed every spring accentuating their well groomed front yard. The boys came in a little dirty from running through ditches and up hillsides along the nearby roads trying to catch frogs and lizards. Each one came in with smiles on their faces. My dad's smile was happiest of all, though, I believe.

As everyone was sitting back in their chairs overfilled with a family favorite, broiled bologna and cheese rolls, chips and dip, and mom's oatmeal raisin cookies, Colleen blurted out, "I got it!" The oldest of my children, Colleen had several years of this tradition under her belt. "Around the corner and up a hill, you'll gain some wisdom and get your fill." Colleen was a typical oldest child, responsible and independent. She continued reading the rest of the note, "Signed the Happy Hopper." Barely able to spit out the words, Colleen read the note aloud beaming with excitement. The clue was discovered taped under her plate. She noticed it when she began to pick up the dishes from lunch. Clearly marked *clue #1,* she knew it was time for the treasure hunt to begin. Everyone's attention was on her.

"Let me see, let me see!" Seany called out, while reaching over to grab the first clue to the treasure hunt from Colleen's hands. Colleen willingly let go of the note, already figuring out what it may have been eluding to. This by far was the most fun for them. Each year my dad indulged in a little clever clue making. The older kids began to try to figure out what corner and what hill the clue was referring to, while the little ones tagged along waiting for them to figure it out for them. We parents scrambled to find our camcorders, so we could record the event.

Colleen was very intelligent and it didn't take her long to start running in the right direction. She left the dining room and around the other side of the wall was the living room with a solid wall of bookcase. She knew grandpa and grandma like to read. "This must be what the wisdom was referring to," she began to think. "But a hill," she thought to herself, "what hill?"

The other kids ran wildly around the living room following her, looking under couch pillows, behind the television, and everywhere something could be concealed. That second clue was elusive though and continued to remain hidden.

Then Colleen's heart skipped a beat as she noticed the mound of magazines and newspapers in the magazine rack. "A hill!" she thought, being careful not to say it out loud, so she could be the proud finder of the second clue. Sure enough, as she began to dig into the pile, or hill of magazines, she discovered *clue #2,* as it was clearly labeled.

"I want to read it. Let me read it. You got to read the first one!" Joshy called out, looking at his mother for approval.

"Good job Colleen in finding the clue!" I interrupted with enthusiasm. "Why don't you let Joshy read it?" I looked toward Joshua, knowing how important it was for him to get to read the clue.

Colleen didn't take long to open the clue, and had read it already to herself. "Here," she said, tossing it his direction, as she ran off.

Some of the little kids followed her as she took off toward the front yard, while the rest of the cousins stayed to listen to the clue.

"Sometimes it's cold, sometimes it's hot. But whatever it is, what you want, it's got! The Happy Hopper" Joshy read aloud, giggling. "How could it be cold and hot?" he said under his breath.

Seany called out, "I know what it is!" He took off for the garage. As if there was an arrow drawn onto the ground guiding him to the spot, he ran straight to the next clue taped onto the back of the water heater. "I found it!" he gasped. Fumbling with the clue, he hurriedly opened the folded paper, marked *clue # 3*.

So this continued, clue after clue. Each of the older cousins had an opportunity in finding and reading the clues. The younger ones ran along just as excited as the rest. As for the parents, we all watched from a close distance, following with our camcorders and recording every fun filled moment. We were entertained by the creative clues and our children's enthusiasm.

"It says final clue!" Patrick called out. Pat was thrilled to find the last hidden message. Up to this point he had just followed the other children along as they scampered from clue to clue. This one was made for him! It was found along the inside edge of the brick planter in the front yard where he loved to play searching for the big bull frogs that showed up there every spring. When a line in the previous clue read *the slimy jumpers* Patrick knew immediately where to go. He tore open the paper and began to read, "All for one and one for all. When you read this note you'll heed my call." Patrick laughed, bubbling out the words as he continued reading. "There lies a treasure too big to hide, but surely you'll discover it somewhere outside. The Happy Hopper. "It's outside! It's outside!" he exclaimed.

The kids scattered everywhere. Some ran up the street, some ran into the back yard and some ran around the front yard. What none of them knew was that while they were reading the clue, Grandpa and Kim were quietly placing a large box filled with toys, painted like a treasure box, near the phone line input which was on the side of the house. They disappeared before being caught as my dad was careful to place the clues so that there was plenty of physical space between them.

"I found it!" Kirsty called out. She was shy, but she was smart. She knew that the slightest hint in the clue could mean where it would be found. She remembered it said *heed my call* and that was enough for her to run to the phone line.

Part of our preparation for this event involved each of us parents bringing a gift for each of our children.

There was a price limit and they were to be wrapped and labeled with their names.

"They found the treasure!" Kim yelled out to the kids down the street. Everyone came running in. Camcorders in place, the parents videotaped their children opening the treasure box and tearing open their gifts.

"This one's for Camden," my brother Don called out. Don liked to pass out the gifts when the treasure box was opened. He made certain the littlest ones got their *treasures* first and the oldest last. He also loved the tradition so much, that he brought one extra gift for each of the kids himself, wrapping and labeling them all. I think he had as much fun as did the children.

"Be sure to thank grandma and grandpa," I whispered into Patrick's ear. The day was long and the kids were tired. We had a three hour drive back to Petaluma and we had to go to work the next day. Patrick ran up to my mom and dad, as they stood on the front porch, waving good bye to all of the grand children that were gathering into their family cars. He gave them a quick hug and ran back to our car and hopped in.

"Buckle up everyone," Kim announced. He rolled down the driver's seat window and with a big smile waved back at my parents. "Off to home we go," he said to the kids, pressing the accelerator, as their eyelids already began to fall closed and they quietly began to drift off to sleep.

Chapter Eight

Painful Truth

"OH, MY GOD!" VICKIE SCREAMED. She could see the front door to her house as she pulled into the driveway from the driver's seat of her old 1985 Pontiac. "It can't be!" She hurried to get the car door opened, as she fumbled with her other hand trying to get a hold of the grocery bag full of fresh produce she'd just purchased at the store. She briskly walked toward the house and up the stairs to the front porch, staring at the horrible sight in front of her. With her mouth dropped open she froze in disbelief and then called out, "Patches, oh my gosh, are you OK?" She dropped her grocery bag onto the porch and quickly loosened the noose that was tied around her favorite cat's neck.

Patches had been hanging from the door knob. It looked like for quite awhile. Her once long white, grey and black patched fur was now scorched black and blotchy and her paw pads were blistered. "It looks like you have been lit on fire," Vickie said softly, as she noticed the smell of freshly burnt fur. Vickie gently held her in her arms, "Shh, it's gonna be O.K." She gingerly began to pet the cat in a spot the fire hadn't torched. Tears filled Vickie's eyes. She stood on the porch for several minutes, looking over her cat, gently lifting her legs and inspecting her body. Patches was still breathing but Vickie wasn't sure if she would survive. "I've got to get you to the vet," she said, while holding Patches as carefully as she could, trying not to hurt her more.

"It had to be Josh," Vickie mumbled under her breath. Her teeth clinched, she began to fill with anger. Then she called for help, "Kirsty, come out here!" The tears began streaming down her face.

The front door opened and Kirsty and Karley both hurried onto the porch. "Mom, what happened?" Kirsty asked. The two girls stood next to their mom shocked by the sight before them. Kirsty was sixteen now and had been babysitting while Vickie went to the store. "Mom, did Josh do that?" she asked suspiciously, peering at her mom with anger mounting within. Vickie shrugged her shoulders. She wasn't ready to openly admit that Josh had committed such a horrendous act.

Karley stared speechless at Patches. She was the one who had brought Patches home from a friend's house just after they moved to Colorado. Her friend's family decided they couldn't keep the cat anymore. Karley named her Patches because of the multicolored long fur, never imagining in her wildest nightmare that she would become a patchwork of burnt fur one day. Frightened, she asked, "What are you gonna do, Mom?"

"I've got to take her to the vet," she answered. "Was Josh here while I was gone, Kirsty?"

"He was, Mom. I didn't know he was gonna do that, I swear."

"Of course not!" She quickly responded. "We don't know for sure it was him... uh, was he mad?" In Vickie's mind, she was still trying to convince herself that it couldn't have been him, but knew deep inside that it probably was. "What happened?" she asked as she began to walk back to her old well used four- door silver Pontiac. Vickie's hair was long and pulled into a pony tail. She had cut short bangs which she brushed to one side. Her red stretch pants were overlaid with a red and white striped tee shirt, now spotted with a yellowy clear fluid that drained from her cat's body. She had on tennis shoes with matching red socks scrunched down to her ankles. "Get me a bath towel, Karley, please." She stood by her car door as Karley hurried back into the house for the towel. "Kirsty, take care of the other kids while I'm gone. I don't want you telling anyone what happened. O.K.?" she said in a low tone so Karley wouldn't hear.

"O.K. But, what if dad calls?"

"You can tell him, of course. But, no one else," she responded. She wished she had the time to go in and call Matthew, but time was of the essence. She couldn't let Patches die. "If Joshua comes back, don't let him in the house. Do everything you can to keep him out." Vickie began to shake, thinking of the terrible possibilities of what could happen. Her throat tightened with fear, "I've got to go, but I'll be back as soon as I can."

Karley came running quickly out, red faced with the towel in her hands. "Here Mom," she handed her the towel, taking in a quick breath.

Vickie folded the towel in half, rolling up the sides, making a little bed for Patches on the front seat of her car. She carefully laid Patches onto the makeshift bed watching her as she lay limply on the soft towel taking rapid, shallow breaths.

Karley looked through the car window at the cat she'd grown to love, her eyes streaming with tears. "Bye Patches. You're gonna be alright," she said through the glass, "I promise." She waved good-bye as her mom drove out of the driveway.

Ever since Joshua found his way to Colorado to live with his family, Vickie had tried to obtain help for him. She took him once to the Emergency Room when he was angry and speaking the German sounding gibberish. She feared he was going to harm her or the other children. She could see he was feeling scared himself, out of control. She had tried every trick she could to convince him that it was safe to get help, with him finally agreeing to go to the hospital. His prescription medication from the psychiatric institution in California had been used up and she wanted to get him back on his medications. Just as Joshua's name was called in the waiting room at the ER, Josh bolted up out of his chair and ran out the exit doors.

When she'd gone to the psychiatric hospital a few weeks prior they'd informed her that he was an adult and though she was his mother, he would have to voluntarily admit himself. Vickie even tried going to the police when she felt his behavior was threatening. She was informed that unless he committed a crime, they couldn't do anything. Now, he had committed a crime. "Now," she thought, "someone will help him."

Joshua was arrested and placed in a mental institution for his crime. He admitted to burning Patches, stating, "It's just a damn cat."

Vickie visited Joshua weekly in the mental hospital throughout his eight month stay. She always had to suck up the courage to walk into that facility. The sounds, odors and atmosphere always got her. "I have to forgive him," she told herself as she walked up each time, "he's my son."

"Joshua," she asked one visit, "why did you burn Patches?"

Josh smirked, and then said with a strong serious look straight into Vickie's eyes, "You always loved your cats more than you loved me!" Then, as if a switch turned sarcastically evil in his head, he said, "Luck O' the Irish!" with a grin.

Vickie was shocked. She couldn't get past the accusation that she loved her cats more than she loved him. She felt guilt pouring into through her gut, turning and wrenching, as though she had eaten spoiled food. It was the clearest thing Josh had spoken the whole visit. Vickie sat quiet. She didn't know what to say. Her heart felt heavy as she considered how much effort she and Matthew had put into parenting him. She began to spin the thoughts in her mind about all of the times they had to deal with his misbehavior. She thought about how she longed for Josh to have a better life, but it seemed inevitable that problems with him occurred. She felt deep within that they had done their very best and that she had to be strong in believing that. "I'm sorry Joshua that you feel that way," she said softly with a quivering voice. "I've gotta go. I'll be back next week." Vickie turned away, holding back her tears as she quietly walked out of the hospital.

It was from that day forward that Vickie's heart for her son was deeply broken. Never before did she feel so much pain. The hope she had carried for Joshua had always sustained her. But now with the callous unrepentant behavior he displayed, she no longer hoped he would get better. Anger began to build up within her. Not just anger toward him, but also toward God. "How could you expect me to live with a child like this?" She prayed. "He burned a living creature!"

Vickie could no longer burn a candle for any occasion.

"MOM, BE SHURE THIS LETTER GOES TO THE MCCALLS HOUSE" The letter began all in caps, *"I WOULD*

HAVE WRITEN MORE BUT THESE ENVALOPES ARE KIND OF CHEEZY. PERHAPS A POST CARD FROM ME OF THE ISLANDS IN A COUPLE OF WEEKS, PERSONALY I DON'T CARE TO BE-FRIEND THE CITY ANYMORE, TAX SEASON IS SEID TO BE A GOOD BREAK FOR PEOPLE WITH ARMY RELATIONS. CLINTON IS HERE AS I WRIGHT, AS YOU AND I MAY AGREE OR DISAGREE, I WOULDNENT LIVE IN A TOWN THAT CLOSE TO NEW MEXICO." The letter was signed *"Joshua Mitchem."* She turned the page to read what was next; still perplexed as to what Josh was trying to say. The second full length letter enclosed was written to Sean. Vickie tried to track what Joshua was trying to say. This was his first communication from the mental hospital since she had last visited him and she became determined to understand him. She continued to read:

> *"SEAN MCCALL,*
>
> *I AM IN NORTHERN WASHINGTON AWAITING A BOAT TO ALASKA. I AM IN A CAMP WITH SOME OF THE MOST STUPIDIST PEOPLE I HAVE EVER MET. THEY REMIND ME OF THE THREE STUGES OF THE OLD BLACK AND WHITE FILM. THEY HAVE INTENTION TO POISEN THE PEOPLE OF RUSSIA. I AM GOOING TO ALASKA SO I DON'T WANT ANY PART OF IT. SEAN YOU MUST BELIVE IN THE BIBLE, IT HAS SO MANY TRUTHS. I HAVE BEEN INJURTED THRUOUT BODY AND SOUL*

*FROM A NEW MEXICO WAR I DID NOT
KNOW EXISTIDED. I HAVE BEEN OFF
MY MEDICATION FOR A WHILE AND AS
SOON AS I GET TO ALASKA I INTEND TO
HEAL MY MIND ONCE AND FOR ALL.
SEAN I HAVE ALLOT OF RESPECT FOR
YOU. A WAR 20 YEARS FROM NOW, YOU
WILL FIGHT IN. FROM WHAT I HEAR
YOU WILL NOT COME TO ALASKA BUT
A PLACE IN GREENLAND, NORTH OF
MAINE TO HEAL IF YOU GET HURT.*

*THE ROAD HERE HAS BEEN
UNFAIR DUE TO CHINEESE-MEXICAN
TERRORISTS. IT IS NOT AS IF I CANNOT
RECONIZE THEM BY NATIONALITY OF
AS IF I CANNOT TELL A CHINEESE TO
A JAPANEESE. ALL THREE OF THEM
HAD TO DUE WITH 9/11, SEAN. AS
A WITNESS I AM FORCED TO HIDE,
NOT ALLOW THEM TO TRACE ME,
AND NOT TALK IN THE AMERICAN
LANGUAGE TO ANYONE WITHOUT
PROPER AUTHORITY. I KNOW YOU TOO
WELL SEAN, I WOULD GAMBLE ON YOU
HAVING THE LANGUAGE ALLREADY.*

*I ENCOURAGE YOU TO BECOME
ABLE TO READ AND WRIGHT
THIS LANGUAGE, IN A SENCE AND
UNDERSTANDING THAT EAVEN OUR
OWN FAMILY CANNOT UNDERSTAND
IT. SO HOW WOULD THE ENEMY?*

SEAN BE SHURE AT THE YEAR 2024 YOU ARE IN NEW YORK CITY AND ARE KNOWN. THIS WOULD BE "PLACEING YOUR GAMBLES" SO TO SPEAK. ONE OF MY ALLIES OF POWER AND ATHORITY WILL DIE DURING THIS YEAR, SEAN. HIS BRIEFCASE IS TOO FULL OF KNOLAGE AND HIS NATIONALITY HAS RUN OUT OF GOOD. MAY GOD REST HIS SOUL WHEN IT DOES HAPPEN.

BE SHURE TO TAKE THE ORDERS FROM OS'GODIAS OF THE FRENCH, HE HAS A SCOTTISH HEALING POND OR SPRING THAT WILL REJUVINATE YOUR HEALTH.

IM SORY I LOST ALL <u>TRAIN</u> OF THOUGHT, THERE WAS A ATTACK AND I HAD TO BLOW OUT MY CANDLE. MY CAMAFLAUSE IS INTENCLY STRONG AS LONG AS THE <u>FLAME</u> CANOT BE SEEN.

THESE ARE REASONS FOR ME TO BECOME SUPERSTISIUS OF CIRMCUSTANCES: I SPEAK TO YOU THRU WRIGHTING ABOUT HOLEY LAND AND THERE IS A ATTACK DURING THE MIDDLE OF MY SPEACH OF WRIGHTING. THIS IS NORTHERN WASHINGTON AND THE POPULATION OF THE PEOPLE ARE MORE IN NON-

AMERICAN, THEN THE PEOPLE OF WHITE AMERICA.

BOTH OF US BY NOW HAVE CHOZEN OUR STAR'S OF NATIONALITY, THRU THESE STAR'S I BELIEVE WE CAN COMUNICATE TO THE HIGHEST EXTENT OF THE GOD'S, WHO SOME MIGHT BE GOOD AND SOME MIGHT BE BAD AND THE START OF THEISE WAR'S.

IN MY PERSONAL OPPINION, HOW CAN THE LAW PUNISH FOR SELF DEFENCE, OR AND ALSO HOW COULD JESUS CHRIST REJECT US FROM HEAVEN IF WE FOUGHT FOR FREEDOM OF THE LAND? WITHOUT FREEDOM WE ALL WOULD BE IN HELL.

I PRAY SIGHNTLY IN THE NIGHT YHRU MY CANDLELIGHT WITH MY ALBINIAN RED EYES THAT ONLY TURN RED ON (1) TROPICAL ISLAND'S OF ALASKA.

MY PRAYER: LORD THYN GOD, DO NOT SEND ME TO HELL IN THE AFTERLIFE BECAUSE OF SOMEONE ELSES WICKEDNESS. SERVING THY COUNTRY WAS LOVE FOR THE TRUTH OF THY BISHOP'S WHO PROTECT THYN BIBLE.

(1)A MAP WILL BE PROVIDED FOR THOES WHO DO NOT BELIEVE, IT HAS

TO DO WITH THE SNOW AND SUB 0
TEMP."

The letter ended like that! Vickie stared at the last line, re-reading it, *A map will be provided for those who do not believe, it has to do with the sub zero temp.* She said almost too soft to hear herself speaking. "What is that supposed to mean? It almost sounds like a clue from a treasure hunt!" Then, Vickie thought about all of the Sundays Josh spent sitting in church, hearing what she believed was truth, straight from the scriptures. "How could he get it all so confused?" she asked herself, under her breath. "That medication they've got him on has made him whacked!"

CHAPTER NINE

Embarrassment

"WHAT'S THAT?" VICKIE QUESTIONED. SHE chuckled, then quickly got serious, pulling her light brown eyebrows together, straining to figure out what she was looking at. Once again, Vickie had come home to an unexpected sight. This day she had decided to take the maroon colored 1992 Grand Jeep Wagoneer, leaving the old Pontiac at home in case Joshua needed to use it. Josh had been back home for several weeks since he had been in the mental hospital, and being stable on his medication, she had been convinced he was O.K. He gladly drove the other kids to school for her and she appreciated the help.

"Joshua get out here this minute!" she called from the open window of her car. Vickie got out of the Jeep and walked toward her Pontiac. There stood her "family car," as she put it, in the middle of the driveway with a freshly painted silver bookcase now adhered to the trunk! As she leaned in to look closer, she could see that the bookcase was the heavy wooden one that she had dusted just that morning in her family room. Now it appeared to be 'cemented' onto the back trunk hood of the Pontiac. It had a shiny black and red stripe painted over it, continuing up over the top of the car and ending on the front hood. She could still smell the fresh spray paint and cement in the air.

"Hi mom" Josh said, as he proudly walked out of the house. "You like it?"

"What did you do to the car?" She asked, still staring in amazement at the strange attachment and paint job to her car.

"I put a spoiler on it for you," he said excitedly. "It's not all the way dry yet, so don't touch it."

"Take it off right now!" She demanded of him.

"Your car will go faster now," Josh looked at her, questioning her demand. "Why would I take it off?"

Vickie's eyes widened as she moved her stare away from his eyes to the *spoiler* and walked over to the trunk of the car. She could see clumps of cement gushing out around the edges of the two shelved bookcase. The smell of the spray paint was still fresh, and she could see little strips of masking tape still stuck to the old paint along the edges of the red and black stripes. She gently touched the edge of the bookcase to knock it off, trying not to get the paint on her fingers. It wouldn't budge! "Come on, Josh! Take this thing off!"

Joshua stood watching. He waited, seeing she didn't want to get paint on herself and then laughed. "It won't come off now! I used cement so it could stick!"

Vickie blew out a sigh and walked into her house. "That bookcase better be off before I get back out here!" Meanwhile, the neighbor woman across the street from her, Sandy, peered through her front window, staring at the car and staring at both Vickie and Joshua. Vickie felt the stare as she walked in the front door of her home.

Vickie immediately picked up her kitchen phone and called Matthew. She began pacing, waiting for him to answer. He was out of town doing a job in Aspen and was going to be gone for two more weeks. Finally he answered, "Matthew, I don't know what to do! Josh has cemented the bookcase from downstairs onto the back of the trunk of the Pontiac!"

"You've got to be kidding!" He said, feeling helpless in assisting her in the situation. "Did you try to pry it off?"

"I couldn't push very hard, because I didn't want to get the paint on me, but I could tell it was already on there pretty solid," she answered in defeat. "I told Josh to take it off. He better!"

Matthew chuckled out the words, "I will work on it when I get home."

Vickie interrupted, "Get home! Excuse me! Do you seriously think I can drive that car like that for two weeks until you get home?"

"Maybe Josh can get it off before that," he said, trying to calm her down. Matthew considered this another of the many odd things Josh had done and for survival sake had resigned himself to this kind of behavior.

"Matthew!" she retorted, "I can't leave it like that until you get here!" Vickie felt helpless, "He even spray painted the book case silver to *match,*" she said sarcastically, "the rest of the car," She continued, while perceiving a humorous chuckle from Matthew, "then he spray painted the whole car with another black stripe, like he did to the Impala, except he used masking tape to make it look straighter AND he added a red stripe to it!"

Matthew continued to chuckle a moment. He then settled himself, "Honey, we'll just have to deal with this later. I'm sorry. You can drive the Jeep anyway."

"Actually," she dragged the word out slowly, with her tone dropping, "I can't."

"What? Why?" he snapped back to her.

"That red warning light came back on. Since that happened last time and the car just stopped, I'm afraid to drive it now."

Matthew sighed. "Look, I can't fix anything from here. I will do what I can when I get back."

Out after a Doctor's appointment, the Jeep had completely broken down the last time the warning light had come on, requiring Vickie to call Matthew for a ride home and having the Jeep towed to the dealer to be fixed. She wasn't willing to chance getting stuck somewhere in the Jeep again, so she decided she'd have to suck up the embarrassment and drive the Pontiac for another two weeks... spoiler and all!

"You can drop me off here," Karley said, as she motioned Josh to pull over to the side of the road. She looked over at Nathan and Camden sitting next to her in the car, feeling grateful the she was the first to be dropped off for school. Any time spent in that car was more embarrassing than she could handle. Karley, now eleven and in her mind a teenager already, wasn't about to be seen getting out of the Pontiac. She still dressed in her fancy dresses and matching shoes. Her hair was pulled back away from her face, with long golden brown curls hanging from the back. She had sprayed on her mother's Tatiana perfume before leaving, making it the only thing anyone could smell in the car.

"I can take you to the front gate," Joshua responded enthusiastically, not getting the hint that she didn't want to be seen in the car in front of her friends.

"Just pull over so I can get out!" she told him sternly.

"O.K. Just hold on a minute." Josh responded. He slowly pulled to the side of the road and before he could say a word, Karley opened the back seat door, and slipped out of the car. She didn't look back at Josh, though he waived to her goodbye, and pretended she had been walking all along. Josh watched her and smiled obliviously, then said to himself, "She must be running late. I'm glad she's out anyway," he added, "she smelled."

When Josh came back from dropping Karley, Nathan and Camden off at their schools Vickie met him at the front door. "I have to go to the store. I'll be back in about an hour." She whisked past him to "the car" with dread as she mustered up the guts to be seen in it on the road for the first time. She was happy Joshua liked to drive so much. It enabled her to stay out of the car while it still looked so hideous. While turning out of the driveway, Vickie caught a glimpse of Sandy across the street watching her leave, shaking her head. "How embarrassing," Vickie said to herself.

As she drove downtown to the market, Vickie noticed several people staring at her and the car. She knew that was going to happen, but wasn't prepared for the reality of it. From the people in the car next to her at the stop light, to the older couple walking along the sidewalk, everyone stared. Their eyes seemed to look intensely at the spoiler, trying to figure it out. At last, the ten minute drive that felt as if it were an hour, was over. Vickie had arrived at her destination. She was relieved as she quickly got out of the car in the parking lot at the store.

After paying for the twelve bags of groceries, Vickie headed back out to the car, pushing her shopping cart in front of her. She was dressed in stretch blue jeans with a bright blue sweater top pulled over the top of her jeans. Her mind had drifted from the thoughts of embarrassment that she had prior to going into the store, almost forgetting about it all together. But reality set in as Vickie looked around the isles of cars and spotted her Pontiac. It was then, that she wished somehow she was dressed incognito. That bright blue sweater was an attention getter! "Someone I know will see me, I know it." She reluctantly stopped her cart at the car as she dug into her big black soft leather purse for her keys. The big ball of keys, held together with a chain of cubed white beads, each bead spelling out *I heart cats,* was easy to find, in spite of her anxious rush in getting a hold of them quickly enough that someone wouldn't notice her standing there. The key ring was a gift, several years old, which she intended to take off after the incident with Patches. She looked at the key chain, remembering Patches, and then the *spoiler* on the car. She couldn't help but feel discouraged with her son. She fumbled putting the key into the trunk keyhole and after turning it she was unable to lift the trunk open. She let her hand loose from the grip she had on the ball of keys when putting it into the hole and now with both hands gripping the edge of the trunk, she pulled up with all of her might to open it. "I can just put the bags on the back seat," she thought, as the weight of the trunk forced itself back closed.

Just then a young woman, probably in her early twenties, walked up to the little bright yellow sports car parked next to the Pontiac. She was dressed very hip, as if she was going to meet friends somewhere. Her make-up was perfectly applied with red lined lip color neatly accentuating her full lips. Her tight jeans, fitted low cut blouse, and high heels were worn with flair. Vickie felt overweight, frumpy, and now thoroughly embarrassed to be seen getting into the Pontiac, the *want-to-be* sports car Josh made it into. It had been a habit for Vickie to use the trunk for her groceries, as much of the time the kids were in the car when she went shopping. When she had realized it wasn't necessary to open the trunk, she sheepishly moved her cart to the side door and proceeded to load the grocery bags into the car, trying desperately not to make eye contact with the young woman.

It was Sunday and as always Matthew and Vickie gathered the children together for church. "Come on, let's go!" Matthew said with all of the enthusiasm he could muster up. Matthew was tired. He worked long hours for the company he now worked for. It was new for him to work under someone else's boundaries. He had enjoyed being his own boss in the past, but now had to conform to new rules and new schedules. He was only home for the weekend and soon would be leaving for Aspen to continue his woodwork in their facility.

"I'm not going!" Joshua stated, stepping away from the rest of the family. "Eswist ish os mos Brazillian hoch dowtas ish moff," Josh called out to them as began to get angry.

"What are you saying?" Vickie questioned, as she entered the living room where Matthew had begun gathering the family together. The kids were all dressed in their nicest clothes, the girls in floral handmade dresses and the boys in their dress slacks and tucked in white dress shirts. Josh was wearing a tie-dye tightly fitting tee shirt with white Wrangler jean pants which didn't quite reach the tops of his tennis shoes. He had on a baseball cap, turned slightly to the side.

"Dos ash owdis granish is aff dowtas dos mogs iswusts! Soudas dosh mosis! Sodis!" Josh continued in angry sounding gibberish, spitting the words back at his mother in response to her question.

"Josh, you will speak to us in our language!" Matthew insisted. "Stop that gibberish. We know you're just making it up!"

Joshua was in a different world to himself. He didn't want to be with them, so he just walked away toward the room downstairs where he had been staying, ignoring what his father was saying and mumbling his gibberish.

Camden drew close to his father, grasping a hold of his hand. Now nine, Camden was very dependent upon his father and mother keeping him feeling safe from Josh. He usually didn't say much, but clung to them for protection.

Nathan, a now fourteen year old freshman student, always tried to please his father. He blurted out to Josh, as he too drew close to Matthew's side, "We know you're faking it!"

"Come on, let's go," Matthew motioned to the other kids. "No sense in being late to church." Matthew couldn't see himself with one of his children dressed as Josh was at church, let alone behaving as he was. The struggle to change the situation was too great. He relented in his effort to get Josh to go with them. "It's alright son, leave him be."

The family all piled into the Wagoneer. The Jeep had wooden running boards along the sides and a luggage rack on top. The tan leather interior was nicely kept and the windows were electric and all functioning. This was a suitable car for the family, and now running, as Mathew was able to fix the light problem when he got home. The family drove off looking like a typical happy family heading for church.

Meanwhile, Josh grew angrier. He watched through the front window of the house as the family left. They were gone. Now Josh had the house all to himself.

CHAPTER TEN

hidden Treasure

"I'VE GOT TO HIDE THE treasure before they get home!"
Josh thought to himself. Under his breath he then began
his usual gibberish. Josh looked around suspiciously as
if he was being watched. He began digging through his
mother's jewelry box which was placed inconspicuously
on a shelf in her closet. He could still smell the Musk
his father ritualistically put on just before leaving for
church, saturated in his clothing hanging next to where
the jewelry box was kept. Most of what was inside was
costume jewelry, just enough to doll his mom up for
church. But, also there were real half karat diamond
earrings used for special occasions, that his mom had
kept for many years tucked inside in a little white box
inside the jewelry box itself.

"Diamonds!" Josh said, as his eyes lit up in excitement
when he opened the little box. "I got diamonds for a

treasure!" He stared at the sparkling earrings, leaving them sitting on the white fluffy padding inside the box. He put the lid carefully back onto the little box and closed the jewelry box putting it back where it had been kept. With the little white box now held closely to his chest, he skipped out of the room. "Now, I have to put it away safe, so no one can get it."

Josh quickly headed out of the house to an abandoned house about a mile away that he frequently went to when he wanted to get away from everyone. He picked up a large pointed stick that was lying on the ground in the back of the house. He began digging with the stick, repeating "I got a treasure. I got a treasure." He dug a hole about a foot deep and carefully placed the little white box into it. Looking all around him and checking to see that no one was watching, he quickly filled the hole back up with the dirt burying the earrings within.

Josh hurried back to his parent's house. The Pontiac was parked in the driveway, spoiler and all. He suddenly got an idea. "The race car needs his number," Josh said to himself. He then began mumbling in his gibberish with a rapid pace, "Dos yos gondis tos dosh pasnish grasis az? Dosh ash dos his tos shaskis..."

While mumbling, Josh went into the garage and found some florescent green, pink and yellow colored tape left on top of the workbench. He began to tear the tape into pieces, applying them in the shape of a "42" onto the back trunk of the progressively more and more strange looking Pontiac. The number was large and he placed it over the whole span of the trunk lid, even on top of the black and red stripe that he had painted on before. He put the extra florescent tape back into the garage and then spotted a can of black spray paint under the workbench in the back. He'd forgotten he had hid it there after he painted the stripe onto the car a few months earlier. Still mumbling his gibberish, he picked up the paint can and walked to the back of the poor old Pontiac and carefully painted "666" on top of the chrome bumper. "Numbers!" he clearly spoke, "Now it's a real race car!"

Sandy, across the street, happened to come out to her driveway to pick up her newspaper. She noticed Josh spray painting the numbers onto the bumper. "What a weird family," she said to herself, "they must be satanic!"

Sandy was pale skinned, sixty five, and very thin. She dressed as if she was already ninety. Her clothes were worn, old, and severely outdated. Parkinson's had begun to set in and her head shook slightly whenever she spoke or even thought hard about something. She looked at Joshua disgustingly, her head shaking more pronouncedly than usual, as if to emphasize her thought, "That man better stay away from my house," pointing his direction with her pale, skinny index finger, "or I'll call the police on him!"

Joshua looked toward Sandy for a moment, then back at the Pontiac. He didn't care that she was looking at him. Josh just stood back and admired the new addition to his car.

"We can just let him keep the Pontaic," Vickie explained to Matthew over the phone. "He wants to move out and I really don't want to have anything to do with that old car ever again."

"Do you think he can handle living on his own?"

"You know," she responded, "he gets the money from the state now and he's twenty years old, for goodness sake. He can take care of himself."

"All right," Matthew said, once again feeling the frustration of being far away from home at work and unable to help as he would have liked. "Make sure you take it out of our name, though, I don't want any part of the legal responsibility of that car."

Good thinking," Vickie responded. "I will do that before I even tell him he can have it."

When Vickie had seen the Pontaic after they returned from church that day, she began to realize Josh was truly mentally ill, that he had really lost any sense of reality. She'd always told herself before that Josh was pretending to behave strangely just to get attention. She convinced herself that the illegal drugs he had taken in the past were the cause of his misbehavior. She truly believed Josh would get better if he got off the illegal drugs. She had felt that when she and Matthew got him back into church he would "see the light" and get on track with life. But when they returned home from church that day, to find the numbers written on the vehicle, she began to believe that he was, indeed, mentally incompetent.

Josh continued speaking in his gibberish in front of the family and while he was alone. The way he dressed and behaved seemed only to be getting worse.

"Here is twenty dollars," Vickie said as she handed the money to Joshua. "You will need to use it to put gas in the tank. It's pretty much on empty right now. It may not even make it to the studio." Vickie had helped Joshua get his first studio apartment for himself. She arranged for the state check to continue to arrive at her house so she could help him manage the money. She and Matthew formed an agreement with Josh, that if they helped him to live on his own, they could have a set of keys to his apartment in case of an emergency. Now, she was officially giving the Pontiac to him along with the money to fill the tank.

"Thanks Mom!" Josh said excitedly.

Vickie and the other kids gladly helped Josh move his belongings into his new apartment. They were excited about him moving out, as now maybe their lives could get back to normal. "I'll come by to visit you next week," Vickie said, as Josh hopped into his race car and drove off.

Joshua drove straight to his favorite gas station. It was white with green trim and was called *Shamrock*. He put in the whole twenty dollars worth of gas. As it poured in, he took in a deep whiff of the gas fumes and said to himself, "Luck O' the Irish!"

It seemed like the week flew by. Vickie happened to be in Josh's part of town and decided to drop by for a visit. She looked around the parking lot while pulling in to see if the Pontiac was parked in Josh's spot. It wasn't. "Hum," Vickie said to herself. "I wonder where he is?"

She began digging in her purse, while getting out of her car, looking for the extra key she had to his studio. "Here it is," she said to herself."

As she approached his door she smelled fresh paint. "Uh ohh…" she thought. The many possibilities of what could be painted began running through her head. "What did he paint now!" she said quietly to herself as she turned the key in the door.

"Oh my Gosh! This cannot be! What has he done?" Vickie stood stunned, staring from the doorway. Everywhere she looked was spray painted fluorescent green; the walls, the little chair and table she had given him to eat off of, the sides of the television, even his small used couch she had bought him from a garage sale in her neighborhood. On one wall he had a big black painted round symbol of some sort. It had numbers coming from the outer ring, with smaller rings drawn inside. It looked like a strange compass of some kind. When she began to walk through the small room, she noticed the dresser. It too was painted green and had an unusual odor coming from it. Her mind numb, stuck in disbelief at what she was seeing, she robotically reached out and opened a drawer. "I wonder what he has hiding in there?" she thought. Her eyes were wide open and her mouth dropped open as she pulled open the drawer. "What?"

There were no words. Out of a huge pile that filled the drawer, Vickie picked up a diaper with torn silver duct tape sticking on each side. And sure enough, it was urine soaked. The stench was intolerable; Vickie quickly covered her mouth and nose as she dropped the diaper back into the drawer. She quickly shut the drawer and ran out of the studio slamming the door behind her. She gasped for air as she walked a fast pace toward her car. Just about ready to vomit, she held her stomach, rubbing it with her fingertips. "Those diapers must have been collecting there all week," she said under her breath. "What do I do now?" she thought. She got back into her car and headed home.

"Mom you'll never guess who we saw today, walking down the boulevard," Karley said, holding back a laugh. They always referred to Pueblo Boulevard as *the boulevard,* since it was a main passageway through their city that everyone utilized.

"Do I want to know?" Vickie responded, still trying to get over what had happened just a few hours earlier, with one hand on a potato and the other holding the peeler.

"Mom it was Joshua. He was wearing a big diaper taped on the sides with duct tape over his pants and..." she emphasized the *and.* "He was sucking on a pacifier!"

"What?" Vickie questioned, as she stopped peeling the potatoes she had begun to prepare for dinner. She put down the peeler and turned back to look at Karley, "How did you see him? Were you in a car?"

"Yeah," Karley said with a chuckle. "I was riding with Jennifer. I ducked down and hid myself in the back seat after I spotted him. Jennifer's mom was driving. We all saw him."

"Oh my gosh," Vickie said, picking up the peeler again. She turned her back to Karley as if to hide her embarrassment.

"Don't worry, I didn't tell 'em that it was Josh," she reassured her mom, picking up on her feelings. "We drove past too fast and he had on a baseball cap so it was hard to see his face."

"That's really weird. I wonder why he was wearing a diaper!" She said while shaking her head. She just wanted to go far away and hide herself. She felt like she could never be seen in public again, for by now everyone must have seen him. She finished peeling the last potato and pulled out a knife to begin to cut them up. "You say they didn't know it was Josh?"

"Seriously mom. They didn't." Karley walked up to her mom and patted her softly on her back. "Don't worry, he's gonna be O.K." Karley wanted him to be alright. She was beginning to enjoy the freedom in her home now that he was gone. She quietly walked out of the kitchen.

Vickie looked back and saw that Karley had left the kitchen. She began cutting the potatoes. "Heavenly Father, what do I do now?" she whispered under her breath.

Chapter Eleven

Understanding Family

"Why don't we ever see Grandma and Grandpa Johnson?" Camden asked Kirstey while sitting in his room on his bed.

Kirstey sat next to him, helping him with his homework, "We need to focus on your spelling words," she said, attempting to refocus his attention.

"I know," he said sadly, "but, I want to find out about my grandparents," he insisted.

"Why the sudden interest?" Kirstey asked.

"I don't know," he said, pausing. Then he blurted out, "I heard Josh talking about them."

"What now!" Kirstey said, taking a deep breath. She almost didn't want to know the answer, "What did your cra...uh..." she stopped herself, "brother...have to say about grandma and grandpa Johnson?" She then wondered, "When was Joshua here?"

"It was yesterday. He just talked about the money," he said looking down.

"What money?" Kirstey asked.

"I don't know," the innocent little boy answered. Camden couldn't remember if he had ever seen them before and only knew of those grandparents because of the birthday and Christmas presents he faithfully received every year from them. "Joshua said they have millions of dollars. That they're rich." Camden began to play with his pencil, rolling it between his fingers.

"Look Camden," Kirstey quickly responded, "you have to take what Josh says with a grain of salt."

"What does that mean?" he asked, putting his pencil down, and looking up at her.

"You can't believe everything Joshua has to say," she said, clarifying her remark. "You know," she continued, "Josh says a lot of things that, uh, well, aren't quite right."

"But why does he say they're rich?" he continued. "There *has* to be a reason."

"Alright, I'll give you that," she said, trying to rationalize the comment. "Yeah, I think they have money, but they have it invested. Like, they don't have tons to spend or anything, they just have money in the stock market."

"What's the stock market?" he asked, prodding for more information.

"Look Camden, you really need to study. We can talk about this another time." She grabbed the pencil from his lap and placed it into his hand. "Now," she said, "tell me how to spell *cautious*." She pronounced the word slowly. "Then write it."

"Mom," Kirstey interrupted, "what *really* happened with Grandma and Grandpa Johnson?"

"Are you asking why we rarely see them anymore?" Vickie noted Camden pretending to study as they talked.

"Yeah," she continued, "what was the big ordeal? You know, the thing that made you guys stop visiting them? We used to go *all* of the time when I was little."

"Well, we lived closer to them then," she said reluctantly. Vickie knew this conversation was going to open a can of worms. "They are in California and we are all the way over here in Colorado. That's enough of a reason to not see them, don't you think?"

"Mom," Kirstey said dragging it out, "that's not what I'm talking about. We stopped seeing them before we even moved here."

"O.K. you got me," she said breathing out a hard breath. "This is a sore subject for me, so bear with me," she stated, while staring out past Kirstey, recalling the event in her mind.

Kirstey looked at her mother intently. She had grown up and was becoming an intelligent young lady. The family was very important to her and with all of the difficulty she had experienced with her brother, she learned very young to stick to the truth in life or life could take her for a ride. "Was it Christmas?" she asked, "Was it that big Christmas that year?"

Vickie didn't say anything for a moment. She could remember the deep pain she had felt that year. Her eyes glassed over with the start of a tear, a lump formed in her throat, she could hardly say the words, "I just wanted it to be the whole family together. That's all. The whole family." The tears welled up in her eyes, and then began to fall down her cheeks.

"Why didn't we go mom?" Kirstey asked softly, with compassion.

"They didn't," she began, then shook her head, "they didn't want us there if Joshua was coming too." Vickie's eyebrows pulled together, she swallowed hard, overcoming the huge lump in her throat. "I just don't know why they had to make it like that! We are all a family. We can't do Christmas at Grandma and Grandpa's house, leaving one of our kids home! That's just not right. Joshua wasn't even…" she stopped. She began to cry, "I miss them so much! I wish they wanted me!"

Kirstey patted her mom's shoulder, "Mom, they want you. They love us."

"Kirstey," she stated firmly, "parents are supposed to understand. They're not supposed to cut you off. They're supposed to do everything possible to make things work out right!"

Kirstey backed off. She could see she went a little too far with her questioning. "I'm sorry Mom," she said sincerely, "I didn't know you felt that way."

"I'm sorry too," her mom said back. "I'm sorry my parents have shut our family out and I'm sorry I, yeah, I'm sorry I unloaded on you like this." Vickie's tone softened. "I'm sorry Kirstey. I love you so much. I pray I never shut you off. Ever." It was quiet a moment, then

Vickie said as she thought about the whole conversation, "Whatever made you think about this, anyway?"

"Oh, nothing really," she said, trying to back out of the conversation.

"Really," her mom repeated, "what brought this subject this up?"

"Camden overheard Josh talking about them," she said softly, feeling bad for bringing it up to her.

"Camden?" She asked, turning her attention briefly to Camden, then back to Kirsty, "What did he hear?"

"Really Mom, it was nothing," she said quickly, turning away and walking toward the front door. "I gotta go, Mom, really."

"Kirstey, you wait one minute," she said as she reached out for her arm, pulling her back towards her. "What did Josh say?"

"He was talking about how they were rich and Camden overheard him," she said, getting her composure back.

"Rich? Huh!" she said with a smirk. "I would hardly consider my parents rich."

"Well, don't they have a lot of money in the stock market?" Kirstey asked, with anticipation. She always thought they did have money and deep down had hoped one day she could somehow benefit from it.

"Seriously," she said hopelessly, "the money they have will most likely get used up with medical expenses in their old age. And," she continued, "if we ever got anything, it wouldn't be much! Who knows, with the way things are between us, we may not get anything at all!" She thought about the studio and the madness of it being painted green everywhere. The next thought was of Joshua walking down the boulevard wearing a diaper. "Maybe it *is* better for mom and dad if we stay away from them. They don't need to think worse of us," she whispered to herself.

"I gotta get my money. I gotta get my money. I'm feeling kinda lucky. I'm gonna get some money." Joshua repeated the words over and over again as he dug through a box he had hidden behind a fence in a dirt lot a few blocks from his parent's house. Inside the box was jewelry he had taken from his mom, his sisters and anywhere he could get a hold of it. The fourteen karat gold was mingled with the costume jewelry and it didn't matter a bit to Josh. He felt it all was priceless and it all could make him rich. The necklaces hung from his fingers as he pulled them out from the mixed up pile in the box. He spotted a diamond ring, and instantly then dropped the hand full of necklaces back inside the box. He picked up the ring and held it to the sunlight. "Look at the sparkly diamonds," he said repeatedly to himself. He gave the ring a kiss and then held it in front of him saying, "I wonder what this beauty can get me!" He put the ring onto his pinky finger and closed up the box. He tucked the box back into its hiding place and ran off toward town. "I'm gonna get some money. I'm gonna get some money. I'm gonna get rich like grandma and grandpa. I'm gonna get my money."

Joshua walked into town and went straight for the pawn shop. It wasn't more than thirty minutes and he came running out of the building with a hundred dollars in his hand. He danced around in a circle with excitement. "I got my money!" he said, waving his hand full of twenties in the air.

People passed by and watched him as he danced around waving the money in the air. Josh was dressed in a Kelly green shirt and tight black jeans that just cleared the top of his socks. His hair was greasy and hung in clumps. His face was unshaven, with a scarce beard forming. He talked to himself as if no one else was around. No one else mattered to him. His money was all that mattered at that moment. "Now I'm rich like grandma," he said with a twirl around balancing himself on one foot.

"Now I can buy my race car. Now I can buy my race car. Now I can buy my race car." He continued repeating to himself, as he happily ran down the street and back to his parent's house.

The Petersons had no idea that Joshua had stolen the valuable jewelry. They had no idea to the extent he obsessed about riches and their grandparent's money. The Petersons wouldn't understand, not for a long time.

Chapter Twelve

Stranger

"I WANT TO GET MY check sent to my house!" demanded Josh, as he came by to talk to his mom. Vickie was sitting on the couch in her living room resting. She had just finished folding the laundry, comfortable in her grey sweat pants and dingy white baggie tee shirt, and was about to lay back and take a nap. Patches jumped onto her lap and she began to pet her.

"Joshua," Vickie replied, as she stood up, knocking Patches off her lap. She tried quickly to think of a way to break the news, "I've got some bad news," she began, "Since your father and I are signed on your lease for your studio, the rental office contacted us."

Josh interrupted, "Those people are weird. They always follow me around. I think they are spies sent from the CIA!"

"Uh, yeah. Well," Vickie continued, looking down as she began to pace back and forth trying to ignore the paranoid response, "they've seen some unusual activity around your place and decided to go in and check it out."

"I knew it!" he interrupted. Josh began to speak his gibberish, "granish tosnish os gosh poff os es gas..." A freaky stare began, as he looked at his mother.

"Josh, knock it off," she said while he was indulging in the gibberish. She flashed on the look Richard gave her before he had raped her years ago, it was eerily the same. She snapped out of it quickly, "I need to talk to you about this."

Josh's voice began to raise, "Dish gas caus faaus!" He spit the last word at her, while pointing his finger down hard to the ground. Josh was dressed in his white Wrangler pants, pulled up high and tight with a belt. His plain yellow-green tee shirt was too tight, as it pulled around his arm pits. He had on his Nike tennis shoes, still in decent condition.

"He almost could pass as a normal kid his age, just looking at him" Vickie thought, as her mind drifted again for a brief moment. She then turned straight toward him, looking him in the eye. "Where are you Josh?" she asked, touching his chin with her thumb and index finger. She began to remember Josh as a child when he could carry on a regular conversation. Now, he had become a person she didn't even know.

Josh reached up and brushed her hand away, "What are you gonna do?" he asked.

"Oh," Vickie quickly replied, getting back to the subject she intended to talk to him about, "uh, the people at the rental office went inside your studio and saw that you had spray painted it." She hesitated as she thought about what she had seen when she went inside and now realizing that they had seen and most likely smelled the same. "They said you have broken the lease, Josh," she continued. "They want you to move out."

"What do you mean? We're allowed to paint it. You paint your house!" he quickly argued. "They're kicking," Josh kicked the side of the couch, "me out?"

Vickie never admitted to Josh that she had gone into his studio when he wasn't home. She feared his reaction so she avoided the whole topic. Josh had only been in the studio three weeks and was already getting kicked out. She knew he would be back in her home with the rest of the family once again. This was difficult for her to think about, but she had to face the reality. Shortly after she received the call from the rental office, she and Matthew held a family meeting with the other children to discuss the situation. Though they understood the reason Joshua would have to move back into their home, the other kids were upset. Each one of them had a story to tell of how Josh's behavior had adversely affected them personally. Vickie's heart broke for them. She felt trapped in her situation. Matthew stood by her, supporting Josh however he had to.

"Even though we own this house, Josh," she responded, thinking she could reason with him, "we still have to follow rules about how we paint it."

"They're probably watching you too. They'll probably kick you out too," he said. "I think they have the house wired. They even listen to our phone calls," he continued. "I hope to never live here again."

Vickie thought about that for a moment. "Where do you think you should live, Joshua?" she asked, wishing deep inside that he had a better alternative.

"I've been thinking about going to Idaho," he answered.

"Idaho?" Vickie was surprised by his response. "Why Idaho?"

"Duh!" he responded, as though she didn't know the obvious, "it's the best place for reception!"

"I know if I put it up I will hear better," Josh mumbled to himself, as he climbed up the ladder he had leaned against the side of the garage. He carried up a fishing pole to the roof and placed it inside the metal trash can he had also placed there. "I think it should face north," he said, adjusting the fishing pole. "Yeah, it just needs to go a little this way." Joshua kneeled on the roof for about fifteen minutes, turning the fishing pole into all different directions until he finally settled on it facing north. "Oh, I need the satellite." Josh quickly climbed down the rungs of the ladder and grabbed hold of the trash can lid, putting it under his arm. With the other hand grabbing the rungs of the ladder, he climbed back up to the top and onto the roof. He placed the trash can lid upside down next to the trash can. "Yeah, that should work," he said proudly to himself. He looked at it for a minute then hurried back down the ladder.

Sandy, from across the street, came out of her front door when she had noticed Joshua putting the trash cans on the roof, pulling her husband Harold along with her. In her shaky voice, she said, "Honey, I told you that family was nuts!" trying to convince him that all of the stories she had been telling him about the Peterson family were true.

"Well, ya have to admit," he responded, in his old, weak and gruffy sounding voice, "that's a bit odd." He gazed for a few minutes with Sandy at the trash can with a fishing pole sticking out from the opening and the lid next to it on the roof. "Come on, dear," he said tugging her hand and turning back toward the front door, "it's really none of our business."

A few minutes after Sandy and Harold went back into their house, Vickie and Nathan, Karley, and Camden pulled up to the house in the Jeep. Vickie had just picked the kids up from school and was talking with them about how their day went. Before they pulled into the driveway, they all noticed the trash can on the roof. The conversation stopped abruptly as they all stared.

"What has he done now?" Vickie asked.

"He's a freak," Nathan responded.

"Make him move back out," Karley added.

"Why is the trash can on the roof," Camden asked his mother.

"That's a good question, Camden," she said, trying to stop the thoughts of what the neighbors must be thinking from entering her mind. "We'll find out, though." She parked the car in the driveway. They all piled out of the car and headed up the stairs on the porch for the front door.

Vickie entered the house. She could still smell the fresh baked smell of the chocolate chip cookies in the air that she had made before leaving to pick the children up from school. She saw Josh sitting in front of the stereo, turning the knobs, with his ear up to the attached speaker. "What are you doing?" she asked.

"Shhh," Josh responded, as he put his head in closer, trying to listen to something. "I can hear them," he said.

"Hear who?" Nathan chuckled sarcastically, as he passed them on his way to the kitchen for a snack.

"Mom, you gotta do something," Karley interjected, as she walked up next to her mother. "He's lost his mind."

Camden walked up to Josh and asked, "Can I hear too?"

Kirstey heard them from her bedroom and came out to see what was happening. "What's going on?" she asked.

Vickie tried to pull her thoughts together. She fully realized what was happening. She deduced that the trash can with the fishing pole were put there by Josh as an antenna. All of the kids wanted her to do something and she knew that she had to. "Josh," she tried to get his attention, "why did you put the trash can on the roof?"

"Why do you always blame me for everything?" he asked. "It could have been one of the others who did it," he said, with a smirk on his face.

"We just got home, you dummie," Nathan said, as he passed them with a chocolate chip cookie in his mouth and another in his hand, heading for his bedroom.

"Why would we," Karley joined in, emphasizing the *we*, "put a trash can on the roof?"

"I can hear the aliens," Josh responded as he continued to listen with his ear to the speaker. Their responses didn't bother him.

"I want to hear the aliens too," Camden said, pulling on Joshua's shirt sleeve. "Can I hear?"

"Shhh," Josh said, as he pushed Camden out of his way. "They're giving me very important instructions."

Vickie interrupted the conversation that seemed to get quickly out of control. "Josh," she said sternly, "I want you to go get the trash can off of the roof right now!"

"OK, jeez," Josh said in return. "You don't even understand, but I know why," he quickly reassured himself. "They told me you wouldn't." Josh reluctantly left the room and went outside to take down the trash can and lid and the fishing pole. While he walked he said to himself, "I should just go to Idaho."

Chapter Thirteen

Getting Religion

"He wants to go, Matthew," Vickie argued as she tried to convince him that Josh would gain from going back to church.

"You know what happened last time he went! Remember?" he responded. Matthew flashed on the embarrassing moment when Joshua came into church during Sacrament wearing at least ten green plastic beaded necklaces around his neck and six inch metal crosses hanging from his ears. The metal crosses were meant for necklaces but Josh had made them into earrings. Every one of his fingers were adorned with plastic rings he had gotten from a gumball machine. He recalled the looks he received when Joshua began clicking all ten rings onto the back of the chair, rolling them over and over again, in front of where he was sitting, distracting everyone in the area around them from hearing the speaker. "He doesn't listen. He won't get anything out of it," he continued.

"But," she insisted, "what if he does get something. Even a little is better than nothing," she said, trying to convince herself as well that it was possible for Josh to think rationally enough to get something out of a church message.

"I guess you're right about that," he gave in. "A little is better than nothing," he said unenthusiastically.

Several weeks had gone by. Joshua continued his unusual behavior, but he voluntarily went to church with the family. Vickie noticed he was reading the bible every evening, highlighting as he read. He was so committed to reading it, that he just about buried his head into the book with a serious intent, highlighting fiercely. She felt encouraged that he had become interested. It was the fourth of July, and a Sunday. Josh had been driving himself to church, arriving at will. This worked best so that the rest of the family could get there without being late. Joshua had just turned twenty one and had been taking his medication regularly.

"Matthew," Vickie whispered behind her hand to him, "don't look right now, but Josh just walked in." Matthew and Vickie were sitting together, dressed in their typical Sunday attire, Vickie in a dress and Matthew in his grey slacks and white dress shirt tucked in neatly. Again it was during their Sacrament segment of the Sunday ritual.

The speaker was giving a moving message and Matthew was trying to listen. "I don't want to look," he whispered back. Matthew tried to concentrate, thinking in the back of his mind it was better to ignore Josh than to give him any attention at the moment. He continued, "I want to hear what he's saying."

It didn't matter to Joshua that anyone wanted to listen. He walked right into the room, bumping people in their seats as he made his way to where Vickie and Matthew were sitting. "Hi," he said loudly, as he sat himself next to them.

Vickie slowly sank into her seat. She tried not to stare, but couldn't believe her eyes. Josh's hair was dripping wet with red, white, and blonde dye still dripping onto his ears and shirt. His hair had a dirty wet smell. "He probably didn't even wash it first," she thought. He had spray painted a sloppy American flag onto his white tee shirt. He had on his worn out blue jeans, stained with splattered paint and grease and had on his Nike tennis shoes. Jeans and a tee shirt were not the proper attire for church, let alone coming in with dripping wet, freakishly dyed hair!

"Joshua, what are you doing with wet hair and dye dripping all over your shirt?" she asked quietly, and then turned briefly around to see if people were looking at them.

With a loud voice he announced, "It's Fourth of July!" looking down at the flag on his shirt with a smile, pointing to the flag.

"Shhh," Vickie interrupted, "keep your voice down."

"Luck of the Irish," Josh replied.

"What?" Vickie said quietly to him, "Josh, just sit quietly and try to listen."

It was the first Sunday in months that Joshua decided to stay home from church. He had been doing better on his medication and decided he didn't need it anymore, so for about a week he had been off entirely. "Everyone's gone," he mumbled happily to himself, "I have the house to myself!"

The sun was bright with the typical August light shining early in the morning. It seemed to call Joshua outdoors. He didn't bathe or even have to get dressed, for he just continued to wear the same thing day and night. He went out the front door, jumped off the porch and landed firmly onto the front lawn. A trailing scent of the freshly cut lawn lingered in the air, as their neighbor had just finished mowing his lawn. He walked over to the tree which grew on the far side of the small, but well cared for front yard. Josh sat down casually, knees bent with his arms wrapped around them. He began looking around the yard at the perfectly trimmed bushes and flowering plants, staring down the street and then over at the garage. Thoughts were racing in his mind. He couldn't connect the thoughts, they just randomly popped into his head. "Green bushes, grass blades, church day, bicycles, gotta be good..."

He began to mumble gibberish as he seem to be talking to someone. He carried on a complete conversation with the invisible person without speaking a single English word. "I know," he then began in English, "there are aliens that tell me what I need to know." He laughed, and then continued, "they look funny with their pointy bald heads and their big eyes, but they're real smart." He seemed to listen for a minute, and then continued telling the person next to him more about the aliens. "I have exact mathematical equations I can show you about the weight and the area of gasoline. They gave it to me."

And then, he jumped onto his feet, ended his conversation with, "I gotta go now." He then began to talk to himself, "I know he's got some wood out here somewhere." He looked around the yard, then walked over to the garage. "Yeah, this is the place," he said. He opened the garage door and started moving stacks of wood around, looking for some long two by fours. The garage had a stuffy stale sawdust smell to it that reminded Joshua of the many years his dad had a wood shop. "Ahhh, that'll be perfect!" he decided, as he pulled five twelve-foot long used planks from the pile. He dragged them over to the front lawn where he began to plot out his project. "Yep, all I'm gonna need is some long nails." Josh knew right where the hardware was located in the garage since his father had it organized fairly well. It didn't take him long to realize he would need to dig holes in order to make his idea work, so he grabbed a shovel from the garage and began digging three holes, spaced about three feet apart, in the middle of the well groomed, very green lawn.

Across the street, Sandy watched from her front window. "What's he doing now?" she said with disgust. "Harold, come and see what the kooks across the street are up to now!" She motioned for her husband with her arm swung back while staring intensely out her window.

Josh tossed the shovel down as he reached for the first twelve-foot plank. "Just right!" he announced. He began speaking his gibberish under his breath, "osh gish ott got dish..." He jammed the plank into the ground with all of his might, "stay!" The board fell right to the ground, bouncing as it landed, as soon as he let go of it. "Crap!" he yelled out angrily.

Joshua quickly ran into the garage and began throwing the once neatly stacked wood off to the side and all around him in his frustration as he dug through trying to find something that would help. "Oh, yeah," he said as he saw three four-foot long perfectly cut four-by-fours. "Just what I need," he said smiling once again.

Josh picked up all three pieces of wood and plopped them down next to where his project was to be erected. He put the tall plank back up and propped one of the four-by- fours behind it, holding it up perfectly. "That'll work!" he said, then began mumbling his gibberish to himself.

He took the tall plank down and pulled out two others from his pile. He then cut the remaining two in half. Grabbing a hammer from the garage he began nailing the short pieces across the upper portion of the long planks, making three big crosses. He carefully put each one into the holes he had dug, propping them up sufficiently with the four-by-fours. "Yeah!" he called out proudly, as he stood back and admired his work.

It wasn't long and the Peterson's made it home from church. As they drove onto their street, they could see Sandy standing in her front yard with her hands on her hips, facing their house, staring. When they pulled up to their house, Sandy looked at Vickie and Matthew in their car, giving them a dirty look. They immediately turned to their front yard and noticed the crosses.

"What?" Vickie exclaimed, as Matthew drove up into the driveway with all four children buckled into their seats in their Jeep Wagoneer. "What has he done now?" she asked rhetorically. The Mormon faith didn't use a cross as a symbol to remind them of Christ's suffering as with Christian religions. It was considered very morbid.

Matthew remained quiet as he usually did when Joshua performed his strange vagaries. He looked at the three crosses boldly erected in his front lawn, shaking his head. He almost wanted to laugh because it was so totally opposite to what he believed, and yet so typical of something Joshua would conjure up to do, he just thought, "in the middle of August."

Kirstey was appalled. "You better have him take those down right away, or I won't even go into the house."

"Why did Josh put three crosses in our front yard?" Camden asked.

Nathan just laughed, as Vickie responded to all of their reactions, feeling the usual obligation and burden of Joshua's behavior. "Alright!" she said strongly. "I'll take care of it!" Vickie fumbled for the door knob as she opened the car door. The rest of the family followed her out of the Jeep.

Dressed in her Sunday best, Vickie walked briskly to the house. Joshua was sitting on his bed in his room reading his bible intently, highlighting as he read. His room was messy and smelled predominantly of Joshua's dirty clothes. "Hi mom," he said straight faced and serious.

"Josh," she began, "Why did you put those big crosses up in the front yard?"

"Hello?" Josh replied, in his usual tone as if stating the obvious, "The resurrection!" Josh began mumbling his gibberish under his breath.

"Josh, it's August," Vickie began to reason with him, "we don't do that," she stooped herself from saying more. She realized it was useless. Josh was in another world.

Just then Matthew came into the room, "Josh," he said firmly, "I need to talk to you." Matthew brought Josh to the garage where a messy splattering of his wood was left. "You're going to pile up this wood back over here," he pointed to where it once was stacked, "and take down those crosses," then pointing over to the front yard.

"NEPHI," Vickie began to read. Vickie had noticed a stack of papers next to Josh's bible, left on the kitchen table. It was written in pencil on college ruled paper and all in caps, "HAD PLATES OF PROPHICY. EVEN THOUGH IT TOOK AWAY HIS OWN LIFE HIS BROTHERS STILL CROSSED THE RED SEA THE GREIT CITY OF POWER DID REBEL. THE HOLY SPIRIT CAME WITH

POWER THE FATHER COMANDED THE PLATES TO BE BURRIED. THE CHILDREN OF THE LORD CAST FORWITH CAMANDMENTS GOLD AND SILVER OF THE LORD TURNED IT INTO MOSES COMANDMENTS. THE ARMYS OF PHAROA TURNED NIGER BECAUSE OF FALLING IN THE RED SEA."

"There's eleven pages of this stuff," she said, as she finished the first page and thumbed through the rest. She set down the stack of papers onto the table and opened up Josh's bible. Much to her surprise, from cover to cover, the entire bible had been highlighted. "Every page," she said as she fanned the pages, "is highlighted." Enunciating each syllable she continued, "Ev-er-ee word!" She stared amazed. The pages were filled with every bright color highlighters came in, orange, blue, yellow, pink, and green.

Breaking her stare, Josh entered the kitchen. "Did you see?" he asked proudly, "I finished the whole bible!"

Chapter Fourteen

Fairy Tale?

"THERE IS A LAND OF AMULON WITH KINGS AND QUEENS THAT ARE DANGEROUS TO LIFE. NURMUS PEOPLE POSSESS LANGUAGE AMONG RICHES THAT MAY PUT THE GAURDS TO SLEEP AND THE PEOPLE OF THE KINGS MAY HAVE THOUGHTS IN THEIR HEARTS. GOOD LAND AND COVIT BONDAGE THAT THEY MAY FIND PATIONCE UNTO GATHERING OF THE DEEP SLEEP SEA. THE LAND OF ZERAHEMLA WILL TAKE THEM TWELVE DAY'S IN VALLY SO THE DECENDANTS CAN MULUK WONDER IN AMAZMENT." Josh began writing intensely. His mind was swirling with thoughts of a far away land where kings and queens ruled and now where he lived. Pages and pages of his college ruled paper became a journal of his adventure. He held his pencil snuggly and continued to write late into the night. The scent of a cinnamon burning candle filled the air.

Asleep, with his head on his last page of his journal, sitting at a small old fashioned wooden kitchen table, Joshua was awakened with his name being called out. "Wha, what? What do ya want?" he said, startled out of his sleep.

"Joshua, honey," his six foot tall and lean girlfriend said, "You slept on the table." She blew out the faintly burning candle.

"What? Oh, I guess I fell asleep while I was writing."

"What are you writing?" Sarah asked, genuinely interested in everything Josh did.

Joshua had been living with Sarah several weeks now since his release from Colorado State Hospital. They met during one of their daily group therapy sessions. Sarah was in because of a relapse also. She too was diagnosed with Schizophrenia; however her condition was managed better. She and Joshua seemed to get along well, discussing everything from their childhood experiences to what they'd been doing to get by in life at that time. Sarah had a job. She worked as a cashier at a Super K Mart around the corner from her apartment. She was thirty and her previous relationships with men had never lasted more than a few months. Though Joshua was considerably younger, she felt they were at an equal level in life and was happy to be with him.

"Oh, it's about the land of Zerahemla."

"Oh, it sounds cool." She quickly responded, "Can I read it?"

"Sure," Joshua said, as he got up so she could sit in his chair, "here ya go." "I gotta pee," he said as he walked away. Joshua walked out of the kitchen and into the bathroom.

"This is interesting," Sarah thought as she began to read the pile of papers in front of her. She had already dressed for work, wearing pressed black pleated slacks and a white blouse, both of which were required by her employer. She wore wire framed glasses which were pushed up snugly onto her thin pointed nose. Her pale skin was only lightly freckled as she managed to avoid the sun as much as possible. Of English descent, she had always considered it necessary to be a good reader and writer, frequently saying to most people she met, "If I am English, I better know how to speak it and write it." She immediately noted the grammatical errors in Joshua's journal. "Oh, my goodness," she said under her breath."

Joshua came back into the room, "How do ya like it?"

"Fascinating story, uh," she paused for a second, then continued, "Would you be interested in someone editing it for you?"

"No, I like it the way it is," Joshua said matter-of-factly.

"Sure, it's good though," she added. She thought briefly for a moment how the story he had written was a fairy tale while she herself felt she was living a fairy tale with him. It seemed to fit. It was the first time she had ever been in love with a man. "Well, I gotta go now. I can't be late anymore or my boss will fire me."

"Can I drive the car while you're gone?" Joshua quickly asked, knowing she would have to leave the keys. She walked to work every day, but her keys were always in her purse with her. Joshua could never take her car for a drive when she was gone.

"Did you need to go somewhere," Sarah asked insecurely. Deep down she always suspected Joshua would leave her while she was at work and she'd come home to a lonely apartment once again.

"Uh, yeah," Joshua answered. "I need to go to my mom's house and get something."

"Oh, more of your stuff?" she said in relief.

"Yeah, more of my stuff," Joshua repeated.

"O.K., here you go." She took off the key to her 1988 Chevy Nova reluctantly and handed it to Joshua. "Don't lose it. I don't have a copy of it."

"Oh, I won't. You can trust me!" he said happily as he pulled out his own key chain from his pocket and added her key to it. "It'll be right here."

"I want it back when I get home," she told him as she walked toward her front door. "I might need to go somewhere, ya know."

"Yeah. O.K." As soon as Sarah left the apartment and walked around the corner, Joshua immediately grabbed his keys and headed for the car.

It was a small grey hatchback, hardly considered a race car, but it got the two of them around. Sarah had kept it in good condition as she never raced it or drove long distances. It was, however, dirty inside and out. The floor inside had piles of fast food wrappers and drink containers. Since she and Joshua had gotten together, her already messy car had become increasingly messier.

"I can paint it," Joshua mumbled, "I will surprise her."

"Josh is here," Karley called out as she looked out her front window from the living room, "and he's driving Sarah's car!" Josh's relapse was extremely difficult on the family. Being admitted to the Mental Hospital was a huge relief to the whole family. It took him away from them and things quieted down in the Peterson home. Karley was happy when Josh met Sarah. It meant he could focus on someone other than her or her family. "I'm so glad he doesn't have that stupid Pontiac anymore," she said under her breath.

"Did you say Josh is here?" Vickie asked while walking into the living room. "I wonder what he wants now," she mumbled to herself. Every time Josh came over since he'd moved in with Sarah, she began to notice that he took things, sometimes things of hers and sometimes things of the other kids. Usually Sarah was with him and Vickie would get a chance to talk with her. She felt overall that Sarah was nice and good for Josh, though under any other circumstance, she didn't feel she would support them living together without being married.

"Hi mom," Josh said, as she opened the door for him to come in.

"Hi, what's goin' on?" she asked.

"Oh, Sarah lets me drive her car now and I want to buy her a surprise cuz she's so nice to me," he answered.

"Come in," she motioned for him to come into the living room. "Are you hungry?" Vickie asked, hoping to distract Josh from where he was headed. She construed that he'd ask for some money. This was beginning to become a habit of his.

"No, not really," he said back, feeling pressured to get to the point of his visit. "I wanted to know if you could loan me some money."

"Here it comes," Vickie thought, "it didn't take him long."

"If you don't have it," he added, thinking he could make it easier for her, "maybe you can borrow from Grandpa and Grandma. You know your parents are rich."

"I'd hardly consider them rich," she laughed.

"Well," he said, "they have a will, don't they?"

Vickie gave Josh a weird look, "What?"

"Just a hundred dollars." he continued. "I'm gonna buy her a ring."

"A ring?" Vickie didn't see that coming. "What kind of ring?"

"Not a wedding ring, Mom," he answered, "just a girlfriend ring. I wanna get her one so she knows she's my girlfriend."

At first Vickie was going to say no, but as she thought about how good Sarah seemed for him and how nice it was having him out of their house since the time she admitted Josh put back into the mental hospital just after his crosses in the yard episode, she relented. "Uh, I'll have to go to the bank to get it."

Josh quickly jumped in, "I can follow you there."

"I guess that'd be O.K." she said, thinking the sooner he was out of the house the better. "Let's go."

Joshua enthusiastically followed Vickie to her bedroom where she grabbed her purse and slipped into her sandals and walked out of the house.

"She's a princess," Josh said to himself while driving the Nova behind Vickie's Jeep. "I gotta get her a ring, then I will paint her car!"

"It's been like a dream come true," Vickie said to herself while driving to the bank, "Joshua has a girlfriend."

"Joshua, where's my car?" Sarah said with curiosity as she entered their apartment after work. She was tired and complained, "Everyone sucks!" She kicked off her tennis shoes, "They never stop coming. Everyone wants to go faster. I cannot keep up with them all!" The store had been busy since the back to school rush.

"Look," Joshua interrupted. "I have something for you." Joshua handed her a fuzzy light blue ring case.

"What is it?" she asked, quickly changing her demeanor.

"Open it," he said with a wide smile.

Sarah opened the ring case and saw a beautiful turquoise oblong shaped stone set in a shiny silver ring. "It's beautiful, Joshua," she said, as she picked it out of its case and placed it onto the fourth finger of her right hand. "It fits perfectly!" She stared at it in wonder. No one had ever bought her a ring before. "Thank you, honey," she said, as she walked up to him and kissed him on the lips.

"I have another surprise for you," he said proudly, feeling pretty good so far about her reaction. "Come on, let's go outside in the back."

Sarah could hardly wait. The ring was such a wonderful surprise and the thought of more seemed unreal.

Joshua pulled her along, holding her hand as he walked her to a place behind the parking area of their apartment building. There was an empty unkempt lot there where he had parked the Nova out of sight from anyone. A few trees blocked their view as they approached the car.

"Ta-dah," Joshua said, throwing one arm out toward the car.

Sarah walked around the trees and saw her car. She gasped. She walked all of the way around it, her mouth open and her hand delicately covering her mouth, looking carefully at the detail in the paint job Joshua had obviously done for her. She noted the spray paint that missed the car and splattered onto the broken asphalt below. The small grey car was now painted black on one half starting from the middle and over onto the side, and was painted white on the other. The black side had big white-sprayed polka dots scattered all over it and the white side had big black polka dots. The front hood had '*Princess*' spray painted in pink in Joshua's cursive. "Joshua," she began, after taking in what he had done to her car, "I don't know what to say." She truly was speechless. She had just received the first ring any man had ever bought for her and truly felt she and Joshua may actually have a chance together. She thought the car looked silly and couldn't imagine herself driving it that way. There were no words that could be said.

"You like it?" Josh asked while waiting for a positive reaction like the one he had gotten from the ring.

Chapter Fifteen

Losses

"Vickie," Sarah said in desperation, "Josh hasn't come back home for three days." Sarah had driven over to the Peterson's house in her *Princess Nova* as Joshua had dubbed it. She had become used to the strange looks from other people on the road and everywhere she went but ignored it all as she was proud to have a boyfriend. "I thought he'd be back and I have been waiting."

"What do you mean?" Vickie asked, "He isn't with you anymore?" Vickie's stomach sunk as she contemplated the thought of Joshua being missing.

They stood in the kitchen as Vickie prepared dinner. She cut up large chunks of Tillamook cheese for the family's favorite homemade macaroni and cheese meal.

"Oh yeah, we didn't break up," she quickly reassured Vickie. "I love Joshua. I want to be with him forever." She threw in, "And he loves me too," as she began twirling her ring on her finger nervously.

Vickie caught on to her insecurity. "I'm sure he does love you," she began as she threw the cheeses chunks into the sauce pan and began to stir vigorously with a wire whisk. "Joshua just hasn't really had a girlfriend before. He has to learn how to behave in a relationship."

"Oh, I'm teaching him," she interjected immediately. "You know, I had a lot of boyfriends before. Well, none as good as Joshua. He's the most special of them all. But, I'm helping him. Like I taught him to," she thought for a moment, "to ask me nicely if wants something. Sometimes he would just take my things."

"Oh, I know about that problem," Vickie said understandingly, bending down to get a large pan for the noodles to cook in. She tried to forget about her missing diamond earrings that Joshua denied taking, and a handful of other jewelry items the girls and she noticed missing over the years.

"But, it's O.K. since we're together anyway," she added. "My stuff is his stuff."

"Well," Vickie interjected, "You're not married. You ought to be careful about that one." She filled the pan with water and set it on the stove, turning up the flame all of the way. "There," she mumbled to herself, "that'll do it." And then, as the thought crossed her mind, she asked, "Would you like to stay for dinner?"

"Uh, no thank you," she responded, and then continued with her point, "But, I trust him. He wouldn't hurt me." The delicious oniony cheesy smell began to waft in the air. "Yeah," she changed her mind, "maybe I will stay.

Vickie felt bad inside for Sarah. She began to wonder if she should have encouraged the relationship in the first place knowing what her son was capable of. "I know you trust him," she said softly, reaching out for Sarah's arm. She patted her gently and said, "So, what happened? Why did he leave?"

"I don't know!" Sarah replied. "We were having fun. We went to the swimming pool at the school. Joshua loves to swim. We hung out there all day."

"That sounds like fun," Vickie said. "Josh is a good swimmer too."

"Yeah," she said in return. "He can beat me in a race across the pool."

"So you like to swim too?" Vickie asked, surprised because of Sarah's almost librarian look. She didn't seem like an outdoors kind of a person.

"Oh, yes I do!" she said with enthusiasm. "I was on the swim team in high school. We had an indoor pool."

"I'll bet you're a good swimmer then!"

"I'm O.K., but Joshua," she added with a dreamy look on her face, "he's a lot better."

"He was on swim teams most of his childhood," she added to her boasting of Josh. "That was one sport he liked.

"So," she began her explanation, "we had to go in because we got too much sun."

"I can see you're a little pink," Vickie said, noticing the skin color for the first time since she had come into the house.

"Well, I had on sun block," she quickly added. "Joshua didn't think he needed any. He said he never had to use it before. I always have though. My skin is too sensitive." She looked down as she spoke.

"So, what happened?" Vickie asked, wanting to find out where she was going with all of this.

"When we got back to my apartment, well our apartment," she continued, "he threw on his blue jeans and his Pink Floyd tee shirt and then for no apparent reason suddenly walked out saying he'd be right back."

"He was walking?" Vickie asked.

"Yeah," she answered, "he walked out. I thought he was going to K Mart to get some Aloe Vera or something to put on his sunburn. But he never came back."

"Sarah," Vickie became worried about Josh's mental state, "has Joshua gone off his medication."

"Oh, that," Sarah took a deep breath. "Well, we had a little argument the other day about that. I was trying to be nice. I really was."

Vickie looked at Sarah with compassion as she knew well how Joshua would get about taking his meds. "I won't blame you for anything, Sarah. I know my son pretty well. I think you have been very nice to him."

"Well, he insisted he didn't need them anymore," she said with a frustrated look on her face. "But I reminded him how we met. We both had went off our meds and look where we ended up!"

"You said the right thing," Vickie reassured her.

"Joshua didn't think so. He just got mad and slammed the door on me." Sarah thought for a moment. "But he was nice again and I thought he was gonna be alright." She sighed and then continued, "I hope he comes back."

Nine months passed. There was no word of Joshua. Vickie and Matthew had begun to worry that Joshua had been killed or died somehow. The police had been notified and said they'd call if anything came up. Then, the first glimpse of hope came. Vickie received a call from Josh's Grandma Mitchem. "Is this Vickie," she said in a quivering tone.

"Yeah, I'm Vickie," she responded, not recognizing the voice at the other end of the line.

"Hello Vickie, this it Richard's mom," she said in a genuinely kind tone. "I'm sorry to have bothered you, but I thought you might be interested in what I have to say."

Vickie's heart skipped a beat as she immediately thought the woman who was once her mother-in-law was reporting her x-husband's death. "What?" she quickly responded, "What happened?"

"I think he's O.K.," she quickly responded. "I received a call from a truck driver headed for the state of Idaho."

Surprised, Vickie realized Mrs. Mitchem wasn't calling about her X at all, but rather Joshua. She began to ask questions. "A truck driver? What do you mean?"

"The driver of the truck called me sounding very concerned," she said in return, "and so he said he'd picked Joshua up in Colorado somewhere where he had been hitch hiking along the highway."

"Oh my gosh," Vickie said, "Where did he take him?"

"Well," she continued, "the driver said Joshua was mumbling a lot and could tell he wasn't quite right in the head. He talked about aliens and, well," she hesitated, "about how he talked to president Clinton all of the time. I didn't know what to say about that. But, he said he tried to get some information from him so he could get him back home safely."

"Good," Vickie interjected, feeling embarrassed about Josh's lies.

"Yeah, well, apparently he talked about me a lot. I don't know, anyway," she continued to explain, "the driver managed to get my phone number from him."

"Wow," Vickie said, very engaged in every detail of the conversation.

"He said he wanted to let me know where he dropped him off and when, so maybe we can track him down."

"Why didn't he just take him to the police?" Vickie asked overwhelmed with concern.

"I wondered that too," she responded, "but he said Joshua insisted he be dropped off in northern Idaho!"

Vickie got the details of the information from her and thanked her for calling.

Later, in early June there was a knock at the Peterson's door. Nathan heard the knock and got up from the couch where he had been watching T.V. and walked to the front door. When he opened it, he didn't skip a beat and just said, "Hi Josh." Then he casually said, "Dude, where have you been?" He briefly looked him over, keeping his comments to himself and motioned for him to come in.

It had been two weeks since Joshua's grandma had called. Vickie had notified the police of his last known location in Idaho, but they didn't seem too concerned about it. She was frustrated and felt alone in her worry. And now, suddenly, it seemed out of nowhere, Josh was back.

Joshua was filthy dirty. He stunk. He obviously hadn't shaved or bathed in a long time. He was wearing the same clothes Sarah had described that he had on when he took off that day after swimming in the pool. He wore his favorite blue jeans and a black tee shirt with a big Pink Floyd symbol on the back and had on his tennis shoes, all worn out and dirty.

"Did I hear you say Josh?" Vickie said as she hurried into the living room from the kitchen. She was so relieved to see Joshua, that she gave him a big hug in spite of his uncleanness. She began to weep, "Joshua, we were scared something happened to you. Where have you been?"

Josh stepped back from her, looking at her, questioning her tears and said, "Why were you worried?"

"Where did you go Joshua, no one knew where you were."

"I went to Idaho," he said matter-of-factly.

"Why did you go to Idaho?" she asked, wiping the tears from her eyes.

"Duh," he began, as if she should've known, "that's where the snow is."

"What?" Vickie questioned. "Why did you need to go to the snow?" She hated the way he always said 'duh' whenever she asked him a question.

"Hello," he said again as if she was dense, "I had a sunburn."

Vickie just looked at him. "I still don't get it," she thought, but didn't want to say anything. "Sarah was really hurt that you didn't call or anything," she continued, taking the attention off of herself.

"Oh, I can't be with her anymore," he stated.

"Why not?" she asked.

"Duh! Because she's Jewish!" he said. "I can't be with anyone who's Jewish! Unclean? Hello."

"What?" Vickie said, totally lost with where he had gotten that idea. She remembered Sarah had been pretty clear about being English. "She's not Jewish, she's English!" she said back to him.

"Not so. She wears glasses," he answered, again as if she should've known.

"I wear glasses Joshua! I'm not Jewish. That's just ridiculous!"

"No, you're not Jewish. It's obvious. She is and so I can't be with her!"

Vickie shook her head, trying to make logic out of his strange thinking and then thought to herself, "Why do I even try. He's lost it." She turned her back on Josh and headed back to the kitchen.

CHAPTER SIXTEEN

pushing the Limit

"YOU'LL HAVE TO HANDLE IT with kid gloves," Matthew said, as he handed Joshua the keys to the 1987 maroon Chevy van that had been parked out back for years. "I don't know if it'll even start," he added. Matthew opened the hood and tinkered with it a bit, wiggling the connections inside. "It's a real gas hog and is practically falling apart,' he said with a chuckle. "But if you want it that bad, go ahead 'n take it," he added.

"Yeah," Josh said, "This'll be great!" Josh needed a vehicle to get around in since he'd come back home and no longer had a girlfriend to take him places.

This had been the family van for most of Joshua's childhood. Matthew hung onto it thinking he could rebuild the engine and use it to haul his wood working equipment and projects if he ever went back into working for himself. But with Joshua's persistence in having it,

Matthew decided it was one way of getting rid of it so he didn't have to look at it anymore.

"Let's see how it runs," Josh said, while turning the key. The engine turned over then stopped.

"Give it some gas," Matthew said with encouragement, not expecting it to have even started.

Josh pumped the gas pedal a few times, "Come on, you can do it!" he said, and the van started.

"Wow! I didn't expect that!" Matthew said with a grin. "Remember, take it easy as it may not stay running long."

"Don't worry I'll take care of it!" Josh said smiling as he backed his way out of the driveway. "Man this is cool," he said to himself, as he proudly drove off.

A couple of days passed and Vickie was driving down the boulevard past Pueblo's *Motorcross Park* which ran parallel to the boulevard. She happened to look toward the park and along with the motorcycle drivers going up and down the hills was her son driving the big maroon van! "Oh my gosh!" she said, trying to refocus her attention on her driving.

The next day Nathan came home from school. He had been driven home by his friend's mom. They had been driving down the boulevard and cool headed Nathan couldn't believe what he'd seen. "A tow truck was towing his van down the boulevard," he told his mother. "and Josh was sitting inside the van turning, as if he was driving it!"

The next day, the same person with the tow truck towed the van over to the house. Josh came out of the van and waived at Vickie as she came out of the house.

"Hi Mom," he said cheerfully, "I put new tires on the van." There were four brand new tires on the vehicle.

"You didn't spend your whole check on that, did you Josh?" she asked, feeling anxious about the obvious waste of money.

"Yes, I did!" he said with enthusiasm.

"Did you get the engine fixed?" Vickie asked. "I can see you're being towed."

"I had to take it out," he said, walking over to open the hood.

Vickie walked over to look inside and was shocked to see the engine was completely missing. "Josh," she exclaimed, "Where's the engine?"

"I told you," he said matter-of-factly, "I took it out."

"Why'd you do that?" she asked, freaking out even more about the extreme waste of money on the tires.

"Duh!" he said as usual, "How can you race it if it has a bad engine?" Josh hopped back into the van which was still connected by chain to the car in front of it. "Let's get goin!" he commanded the driver of the tow truck, as he sat up alert in the front seat of the van, smiling.

"What am I supposed to do?" Vickie asked as she looked up toward heaven, throwing her hands into the air.

A few weeks later, Vickie went outside to get into her car, and there was the van, parked on the curb outside their yard. Josh had painted an American flag on one side and a marijuana leaf on the other. The side with the big leaf on it faced the street, directly across from Sandy's house. "So much for getting rid of the van," she said sarcastically to herself, "I'll bet the neighbors are lovin' this!"

Josh sat proudly now in the front seat of the old family Jeep Wagoneer, gripping the steering wheel snugly as he pulled out of the driveway.

"How could you give the Jeep to Josh," Kirstey asked, feeling it should've gone to her as she would be going to college soon. After all that had happened with the van, she couldn't believe they'd give him the Jeep also.

Deep within, Vickie felt guilty for giving Joshua another vehicle. But, with Josh's continual persistence asking and Vickie's underlying desire to have Josh gone from the house, she and Matthew both caved in with their decision. "We'll try to help you get your own car, but Josh needs one now and we are just loaning him the Jeep until he can get one of his own," Vickie said, convincing herself that it was going to be all right giving him a vehicle once again. She believed the sooner he had wheels, the sooner she could get him back out on his own once again. "Besides," she added, "it's getting so old, the heater doesn't work and the family's really put that thing through the ringer."

"That's just not fair!" she insisted. That guy doesn't deserve anything. All he does is hurt everyone!" This was the first time Kirstey had ever spoken so harshly against Josh. She generally had so much compassion that she could see past his antics and into his heart. But now it was affecting her in a serious way. She needed a car! Since her parents had a new family car, a 2000 Pontiac Grand Prix, the Jeep was an extra vehicle. "It's always Josh! Josh this and Josh that!" Kirstey had had it.

Vickie gave Kirstey a look she usually gave to Josh when he said something outrageous, "That's real nice," she said sarcastically. "Look, I'm sorry, Kirstey, but this is what your father and I have agreed to do," Vickie said emphatically, "besides, we want to help you get one of your own."

"That's a good idea," she said, softening her tone, "but I can't have car payments if I'm gonna go to college."

"We'll work something out," she said, trying to reassure her.

"Josh," Vickie said in a frustrated tone, "get off the phone."

"Shh...," he said as he glanced her way, "I'm on an important call.

Josh had been on the phone for hours. Vickie ignored it for the most part, but when she needed the phone she began working on him to get off. She had listened in on what Josh had been saying off and on as she had passed by him while doing her daily chores. She figured he had been talking to his cousin, Sean, because he seemed to be asking him about a tattoo. Sean had become a professional tattoo artist and several people in the family had gone all of the way to Reno for a personal picture on their bodies. When Josh had found out about that, he was determined to get the flames he had put onto his arm while in jail, filled in with color.

"I can't tell anyone I'm talking to you," he whispered into the phone with his hand cupped over his mouth. "This has to be top secret," he explained, "cuz once the cops know your tattoos anyone can identify you." He continued talking about the details of his tattoo, how he wanted the red, yellow and orange to burst into action in the flames. "You know how to do that, don't you Sean?" he asked.

Vickie passed by him again, "Joshua, you've been on since this morning! Get off now!"

"I can't yet," he explained, "I gotta make sure everything's set up."

Frustrated, Vickie went downstairs to the den where the other phone was located and picked up the receiver. "When can we meet?" she heard him ask. There was no response. Vickie continued to listen, and then Josh said, "Good, I'll see you there."

"Oh my gosh," she whispered to herself as she quietly pushed down the receiver and hung up the phone. "There's no one even there." She sat back in the black swivel desk chair they had at the computer desk where the phone was kept and just thought about the hours he had just spent talking to himself.

"I'm off now!" Josh called out a few minutes later. "You can have your precious phone back!" Josh went to his room and closed the door.

When the other kids came home from school, Joshua heard the commotion from his room as they piled into the house one by one. He began to get nervous, clapping

143

his knees together where he sat at the desk in the room. It wasn't long afterword that he could hear Kirstey playing her keyboard in her bedroom. She practiced daily and it was the time Joshua hated the most. He put down his pen onto the stack of papers he had been writing on and said to himself, "I can't even think with those animals here. I gotta go." He quickly changed out of his tee shirt and put on his dress white shirt. "Gotta cover the tats," he said to himself. He walked briskly out of his room and out of the house, slamming the door behind him.

"What's that about?" Nathan asked, watching Josh buttoning his shirt while leaving the house. "I wonder what the freak was up to today?" He walked into his room where Josh had been staying this time around. He picked up the stack of papers and noticed the first one was a letter and began to read:

"DEAR GRANDPA AND GRANDMA,

THE TEN ACTIVATOR CREAME IS HEALING ME, AND THAT WAS THAT. 10 X 7.95 I PRESUME. ENGLISH MEDICINE IS NOT BETTER THAN TRANCELVANIAN MEDICINE BECAUSE THE COST WOULD HAVE BEEN APX. 320.00. ANYWAYS I THINK I HAVE LEARNED HOW TO HOLD MY TONGUE AS FAR AS GERMAN-TO-ENGLISH AND ALIAN'S ARE MUMS THE WORD. I STILL HAVE 5,000.00 CASH-CREDIT. THESE CHINESE WILL PAY FOR THEIR MISTAKES. TAKE PICTURES OF THEM SPENDING OUR CASH AN WELL

SUE THEM, A CHINEESE LAW SUIT WOULD LEAVE US WITH A EXTRA BANK. MY RADIATION SICKNESS IS SO POISNESS. I AM STANDING NEXT TO MATTHEW (VICKIE'S) BOYFRIEND CHINA AND JAPAN CLAIM THEY HAVE TWO MOON'S MAYBE THEY DO AND MAYBE THEY DON'T. KEEP ON DRINKING THAT HEARBAL TEA IS WHAT I THINK. DARKNESS BE WITH YOU, I SPIT ON YOUR KING

JOSHUA MITCHEM

Nathan began laughing as he read the words. He took the letter as he finished the last sentence and went into the living room where his mom was sitting on the couch. "Take a look at what your son wrote to your mom and dad."

Vickie grabbed the letter from Nathan.

"You can have it," he said. "I can't stop him from nothin'," Nathan concluded. He walked away throwing his hands into the air and went into his room. He picked up his bass guitar, turned it on and began playing random notes as loud as he could.

Vickie began reading the letter. It was hard to concentrate with the guitar so loud and thinking how Josh's behavior was so adversely affecting the other children. "What was he thinking?" she said to herself. She shook her head, "Obviously we won't let him mail this."

"Turn that down," Vickie called out to Nathan.

Joshua drove his Jeep to the Shamrock Gas Station, about forty five minutes from his house. "Is anyone here?" he asked, as he opened the door and walked into the office.

"Yes sir," a kind man in his early fifties with a grey scruffy beard answered, as he got up from his chair.

"I'm lookin' for some work," Joshua said plainly.

"You ever done any mechanical work, son?" he asked, checking Joshua over. Josh had on a nice white dress shirt and a decent pair of blue jeans with his white tennis shoes. The man glanced over at the Jeep, taking notice that Josh had the ability to drive there. Getting responsible workers was getting more and more difficult for him.

"All the time," he answered the kind man.

"I might have some work for you," he said, giving Joshua some hope for the job. "You'll have to fill out an application, though." He reached into the top drawer of his grey metal desk and pulled out the form.

"I can have my secretary do that for me," Josh said, taking the one page application from the man. "Thanks!" he said with a smile. "By the way," he added, almost making it through the conversation without the kind man catching onto his mental issues, "you might want to check for treasures here. I think the gas here might have special qualities that could calculate to a lot of money." He paused, and then added, while looking at the man squarely, "We might have some business at a later time," as he walked out of the office.

"His secretary," the man said to himself, as Joshua left. "Treasures?" he shrugged his shoulders. "Huh, another kook!"

Joshua didn't come home that evening. Matthew called just before Vickie crawled into bed. Vickie walked back out to get the phone from the kitchen when it rang, knowing it had to be Matthew calling. "Hello?" she asked when she picked up the phone. She walked back to her room with the phone tucked between her chin and her shoulder as she finished rubbing in her favorite Victoria's Secret Lotion, Love Spell, all over her hands and arms. Finally, she crawled into her bed. The fragrance was strong. She liked to put it on especially when she was feeling stressed about something. This night Matthew hadn't called from Maryland, where he took a three month job, at his usual time. She needed the strength he provided for her when he called. "

"Hi honey, it's me," he said apologetically. "Sorry for calling so late."

"It's O.K." Vickie answered, holding back her tears.

"What's happening?" Matthew asked.

"I don't know, it's one of those days," she began. "Josh didn't come home tonight. He left after writing a disturbing letter to my parents. The other kids are getting tired of him. Kirstey is missing her ring she just got for her birthday. She blames Joshua. Nathan wants him out of his room." Vickie continued, pouring out her frustrations onto Matthew, while his listened. "They are fine really. There is just a lot going on. Their homework. Practicing. I just wish you were here."

"I can't be there," he said softly. Matthew seemed to feel helpless once again as he was too many miles away to do anything for them. "It is just another three weeks and I will come home. I will give you a back massage and I will even cook for you!" he thought of whatever he could say that would bring her a smile. "I love you. I keep you always in my prayers."

Vickie smiled briefly, and then seriously said back to him, "I love you too." Her eyelids began to feel heavy, as her speech softened and slowed down. "They got the homework done and..."

Matthew interrupted, "What?" he could barely hear her and knew she was falling asleep, "Honey, you better go to sleep, I'll call you tomorrow."

"Thank you," she said, while the last of the words barely came out. The phone fell from her hand and onto her bed as she fell fast asleep.

Chapter Seventeen

Going Mental

"Aaaaaaahhhhh!" the sound of the scream echoed down the long hallway from the Intensive Care Unit of Spanish Peaks, the local mental hospital in Pueblo. "No!" the female voice screamed, "You can't have me!"

Joshua reached over from where he sat and turned the volume up on the television as he watched the popular show, 'Friends' in the activity room. "Gets noisy in here," he laughed to the guy next to him.

"Yeah," he said in response, a little freaked out with all that happened around there.

"Ya new here?" Josh asked the guy, perceiving his skittishness.

Uh, yeah," he said again. "Just in to sober up."

"It's not bad here," Josh began. "They have some food here that I think they poison. They may or they may not. What's your name?"

The guy hesitated in answering, giving Josh a questioning look, "poison?"

"It won't hurt you if you take the radiation therapy. I heard that," he looked at him seriously, "from a reliable source. I can't tell you they're aliens or they will stop their protection."

"Oh, yeah," he said in return, pretending to believe Josh. "Yeah, my name is Roger."

"Roger," Josh said, "the other thing is you have to watch out for the hidden cameras. They're everywhere. They even watch you take a crap!" Josh laughed. "Can you believe they watch you piss and pull down your pants."

Roger just laughed and turned his attention back to the T.V.

"Was as beggas das condas," Joshua began speaking his gibberish as he got up from his chair and started pacing back and forth behind Roger. "Tas as ish is slas..." he raised his voice above the sound of the television.

"I think I'm gonna go out for a smoke," Roger said as he got up from where he had been sitting and walked toward the sliding door which lead to the patio area.

Joshua reached into his pocket and pulled out a pack of cigarettes. He always took up smoking while he was in the hospital. It made him feel like he fit in better. He followed Roger out onto the patio and took a cigarette out and put it between his lips. While fumbling for his lighter, his lips still holding tight, he asked Roger, "Got a light?" His cigarette moved up and down as he spoke.

Roger reached over and flicked the flame on his lighter just under Josh's cigarette. Josh inhaled deeply and then said as he blew the smoke out of his mouth, "Love these Marlboros!"

"Can only smoke the lights anymore," Roger said, stepping back from Joshua.

"You'll quickly learn," Josh began to *teach* Roger, "the cigarettes will give you a power you won't find anywhere else but here."

"Hello," Karley said, as she picked up the phone at the computer desk. She was typing at the computer, trying to finish an assignment for her English class.

"May I speak with Vickie," the pleasant voice on the other end of the line said.

"Sure, I'll get her," Karley responded. She put the phone down on the desktop and yelled upstairs, "Mom, it's for you." She picked the phone back up and listened for her mom to pick it up.

"Hello," Vickie said.

"Vickie, this is June down at Spanish Peaks," she began.

"Oh," Vickie immediately interrupted. She had spoken to June before in the past and really trusted her judgment. "Did Josh get picked up?"

"Yeah," she answered. "We've got him here to get him stabilized on his meds."

"I figured something like this happened. He's been gone for over a week now and we couldn't find him anywhere," she said with a sigh of relief.

"Yes, well, apparently he was stopping people and telling them all kinds of things about the aliens and the secret government plots. He freaked out the wrong person, an off duty cop! He turned him in right away."

"Oh gol," Vickie said."

Josh asked us to call you to let you know where he was," she explained. "Usually we just have them make their own phone calls, as you well know by now, but Joshua is struggling right now. We thought it would be a good idea to call you for him."

"Struggling?" Vickie asked.

"It's taking longer this time to get him stabilized."

"I see," Vickie said. "Do you think it might help if I came down to visit him?"

"It might," she answered. "It probably won't hurt."

Vickie thanked June for calling and hung up the phone. With a glazed blank stare at a bare spot on the wall in front of her, she sat down in the chair at the kitchen table and just stared.

"What are you looking at, honey," the large black woman said with her ghetto accent. She plopped her large bottom down onto the chair in the cafeteria next to where Joshua was sitting. She wore purple stretch pants and an orange and purple paisley jersey blouse. Ruffles along the neckline bunched up on top of her full breasts. "Don't you be eyeballin' my food," she said to Josh, as she scooped a heaping spoonful of mashed potatoes into her mouth."

"That would be a mistake," Josh said to her, "I might have to call for some help." Josh looked over to where he saw a large man standing with binoculars looking at the lady eating. "Maybe you could come over here with me," Josh said to the man, motioning him to come to him.

"Who are you talking to?" the black woman asked. "There ain't no one there where you're lookin', honey!"

"Come here, don't be afraid," Josh said to the man. "She just has black skin," he added, "only she's pretty strong. I could tell."

"You crazy, white boy," she turned her head and quickly started to eat the rest of her food. "There's no one there."

Vickie took a deep breath as she walked toward the hospital with a pile of Josh's clothes under her arm. It didn't seem that long since Josh was there last. "Well," she said to herself, "get ready for the smell!" That was the part she just couldn't get over. She never quite put her finger on what the odor was, but somehow it was stale and stuffy and awful.

She made her way through the hoops of checking in before meeting Joshua at the activity room where he liked to meet her. She avoided the patio area because she didn't want to be around the smokers. "Hi Josh," she began, as she walked towards where he was pacing. "How are you doing?"

"Tos dosh powdas ash has nosh ester," he began, as he seemed to ignore her question. Josh knew she was

153

there but continued to speak gibberish. His eyes stared wildly at her but seem to look past her. He was wearing the clothes he came in with, his jeans and white dress shirt, which had gotten very dirty.

"Josh," Vickie continued, ignoring the gibberish and the freaky stare, as she had gotten pretty used to it. "I want to help you. What can I do to help you?"

"Just tell the president, Clinton, that I have the secret formula for the nuclear atomic bomb," he said clearly, then began gibberish again under his breath.

Ignoring his response, she asked, "Can I get you some snacks or a movie?" She paused, "I brought you some clean clothes." She thought for a moment, "Maybe that's why it always stinks here. All of the dirty clothes." She continued, "Anyway, I wanted you to know I am praying you'll get better."

"What can Moses do? Huh?" he said clearly, then began gibberish again.

"Heavenly Father is there to help you Joshua. Just ask him." Vickie knew by his response he was at least hearing her. She took that as an encouragement.

Just then a short unshaven grey haired man, with missing teeth in front walked in. "Excuse me while I fart," he said, and then let off a long rancid-smelling gas bomb. "I gotta sit over here so I can watch T.V." he said, as he walked between Josh and his mother.

Two women walked in after the man and were talking loudly with each other. The first one was an obviously fake blonde, very thin, with straggly fine hair and a pimply complexion. "I got those too!" she said.

"You do?" the other woman said, also thin and looked very unhealthy.

"Yep!" she said, "My boys and I keep it all good!"

Vickie had no idea what they were talking about, but she was getting very uncomfortable. "I think I better get going," she said to Joshua.

Josh still paced. He didn't even flinch when the others came into the room. They just looked at him as he spoke loudly enough for them to hear his gibberish and they seemed to stay clear of him.

"He's a real nutcase," the blonde woman said as she smiled revealing her missing teeth.

"Ah, he's harmless," her friend said in return, looking Josh over.

"Everyone get down!" Josh suddenly announced as he began sweeping his arm outward. "The Japs are here!" He moved toward the blonde woman, putting his hand onto her shoulder, trying to get her to get down.

"Get your filthy hands off me, you pig!" she said, shoving his hand off of her.

Josh turned toward the short man, "You," he pointed to him, "get down on the ground!"

"You gotta be kidding, you psycho," he said loudly. "Get lost!"

The other two women were beginning to get louder also, accusing Josh and making fun of what he was saying.

It all was happening so quickly. Vickie couldn't believe what was happening. Everyone was talking loudly. "Josh, come here," she said, motioning to him to come to her.

She thought if she could get him out of the room, he'd settle down.

Just then a staff nurse came into the room. She quickly asserted that Joshua had been disturbing the other patients. "Josh," she began, "you can come with me now."

Surprising to Vickie, Josh followed her as she walked him to another room.

Vickie stood in the activity room alone with the others around her still talking loudly about the incident for just a moment. She stood wondering, "How could this possibly be happening to my son?" And then, she walked out.

Chapter Eighteen

Öriving Crazy

"You won't believe what I just saw?" Kirstey said, walking in the front door. It was the dead of winter and freezing outside.

"What has our favorite sibling done now?" Nathan said sarcastically, hearing Kirstey when she came into the house. He had a handful of potato chips in his hand and was passing through the living room toward his room.

"You know how the heater is broken in the Jeep?" Kirstey began.

Vickie came in from the kitchen when she heard the two of them talking about Joshua. "Did you say you saw Josh?" It had been several weeks since he'd been released from Spanish Peaks and Vickie hadn't been over to his new place to visit him yet.

"Yeah," Kirstey said. "He was driving down Pueblo Boulevard in the Jeep and the windows were all fogged up," she continued."

"I knew we should've fixed that heater before loaning it to him for the winter," Vickie said to herself, shaking her head.

"It was hilarious!" Kirstey exclaimed. "I was driving home from class and recognized the Jeep right away, coming from the other direction."

"So, get on with it," Nathan said, standing there, crunching a chip and wanting to get to his room.

"Joshua," she laughed, "was driving wildly all over the road like he always does, only he had his head hanging out of the window like a dog!"

"Oh, brother," Nathan said.

"Yeah, it was funny," she added, "especially since he was calling out random things to everyone passing by."

"So he was driving recklessly?" Vickie asked.

"Mom," Kirstey said, with an obvious tone, "He always drives like that."

"Oh, boy," Vickie said to herself, as she began to open a letter from Joshua. She had just picked up the mail from the mailbox and when she saw the letter addressed to her with a return address from "1 Transylvania," she never expected what she saw. The letter began:

> " I CAST THUS MAJIC AGAINST THE
> HOUSE OF THE PETERSONS"

The top half of the page was covered in a drawing with his writing pen. There were three five-point stars, each within circles. Below each of the three stars were crosses, shaped more like thick plus signs. Below the crosses were flames. Next to that part of the drawing was another drawing, this time of a cloud with six thick drops falling from it. Josh had written below this,

"X Lucifer   X 666"

A simple picture of a house was under that. Below the house began the writing, in cursive:

> "The Chief from the father to the youngest daughter yea will live in a tent and use no utenciles to I am most holy sacrificing 3 priests as you have in the tent it will be no land of Egypt but a dark day for this stone tablet came out of a cloud and filled your house with evil."

The front of the page ended there with the mixed up biblical concoction of stories. Vickie finished reading it and hesitated to read the other side. "What is the point?" she asked herself. But she felt curious about it for some reason, flipped over the page and continued to read:

> "The thickest gloom will leave you sesussfully rebuilding your house and Jehova will be able to bless your younger with capabilitys of fullfullment."

There was a space, then a separated quote written in printing:

> "I have not chozen a city but only one house"
>
> "My name is to be spoken as a trusure of crown of diamonds and emeralds You will have to pray to Jehova the god more then when comantment to save thus curse and altar sacerfice promise Your own mouth you will no longer keep thourad your servant you had better pray that your sins will leaving you walking again and that given possible legs I cast mildew locusts cockroaches thru the gates of the house of the Petersons whenever I think akad thought twards your families- plague-"

It ended just like that. No signature.

"What am I supposed to do with this?" Vickie asked herself. "Any more of this kind of stuff and he will drive *me* to the nut house!", she said, emphasizing *me*. She put the letter down on her nightstand in her room where she ended up while reading the letter. "All I ever did was try to be a good mom," she began, as she sat down onto her bed, talking to herself. "And this is what he wants to do to me!" she almost couldn't say the last thought, "Cast a curse on my house!"

"So what'd you do after that?" Karley asked, popping another French fry into her mouth.

Joshua continued telling his story, "I told her I got connections," he said proudly. Josh was dressed very ordinary in a pair of blue jeans and a white tee shirt. He began stirring his soda with the straw in the little restaurant called *The Village Inn* in Pueblo.

"Oh, yeah?" Karley said with a chuckle. She was trying hard to spend time with Josh and to treat him normally. She was well into her teens now and had begun to understand that Josh was just different. Though Josh was dressed ordinary, he had on several strands of plastic beads around his neck and was wearing plastic rings on his fingers. Karley managed to ignore the attention he drew to himself and focused on having some kind of meaningful conversation with him.

"Yeah, it was funny," he continued. "They puked up their whole meal all over the floor and still wanted to know who my connections were!"

"That's sick," Karley said, barely being able to swallow another french-fry." She grabbed her soda and took a big gulp.

"You could smell the harfed up food everywhere!" he said, laughing about it.

Still trying to keep the conversation going and acting interested, Karley asked, "So who are your connections Josh?"

"I can tell you no lie," he began, "but I cannot tell you the whole truth." Josh bit into his double patty hamburger. While chewing he continued, "There are important people in the White House you know. That's all I can say about that!" With that, he washed down the bite with a drink from the side of his cup, spilling ice onto his plate.

Karley continued talking with her brother until they finished eating. She paid for the meal at the cash register and began to walk with him to the exit door. "Amazing," she thought, "We actually made it through a whole meal in public without making a scene!"

As luck would have it, Josh followed Karley to the door and just as she began to walk through, he turned around facing the inside of the busy restaurant and announced boldly, "I'm a homosexual!"

"Oh my God!" Karley said, rolling her eyes, and covering her face with her hands. She just about lost it. She wanted to go hide.

Joshua smiled and turned to Karley. With an emphasized limp wrist held up, he said with a lisp, "I am, you know. I have boyfriends."

The winter gave way into the spring. It was a rainy Sunday and Joshua surprised them with his attendance at church. There was no plastic jewelry, no dyed hair, and no outbursts of embarrassment for Vickie and Matthew to endure. "Let's take him out for lunch after church," Matthew whispered into Vickie's ear just after sacrament ended.

"Good idea," Vicky said enthusiastically. "I think his meds must really be working," she added.

"Josh," Matthew said. "We'd like to take you out for a bite to eat after church, O.K.?"

"Do ya want to meet out in the parking lot afterwards?" he asked. Joshua had driven the Jeep to church and when he'd arrived, he'd seen saw a parking spot next to the family's new Grand Prix and grabbed it.

"That'd be perfect," Vickie responded. She and Matthew split off to their classes as they always did. Vickie was feeling an air of normalcy with Joshua that she hadn't had in so long she couldn't remember. It made her feel there was hope. She took a deep breath as she parted from them and let it out with a satisfied-looking smile left on her face.

Classes ended and Vickie met up with Matthew and Joshua. They gathered together Kirstey, Nathan, Karley, and Camden and headed for their car.

"Oh my gosh!" Kirstey said, covering her smile, as she walked toward their car.

"Josh!" Vickie exclaimed, "What did you do?"

"Classic," Nathan said, walking faster so he could take a closer look at the Jeep.

"Why'd you take the rack off Josh?" Matthew asked sternly, as he began to look over the Jeep. Matthew began to fill with anger. He hadn't given the Jeep to Josh, it was only a loan to get him through the winter. "That's my vehicle, you know!" he strongly said to Josh.

There were people leaving church who didn't want to appear nosey, but they, too, were looking at the Jeep when they passed by. Matthew turned his back to them and continued with Josh, "I can't believe you would do that!"

"Had to fix it up," Josh said, as if it was much better now that he had painted it.

"Why did you put a rainbow on the top?" asked Camden. "It looks funny, Mom," he said, turning to his mother.

"You don't want to know," Nathan interjected, knowing full well why. For the past few weeks Josh had been making a point of everyone knowing he was gay.

"He put a Pink Floyd symbol on the hood?" Karley said with a question in her voice, adding to the growing description of the hideous looking Jeep. "I knew he was off his rocker, but that really takes the cake!" she said with a laugh.

"Look," Matthew said, looking into the inside of the Jeep. "There are drips of water coming down through the holes he left from removing the luggage rack!" His anger intensified. He began to breath faster. "Joshua," he said, turning to him, "Give me those keys!" A small vein popped up on his forehead, going from between his eyebrows up to his hairline.

"Matthew," Vickie interrupted, "What's the point? We can't drive it now! It's ruined!"

Matthew turned his attention to Vickie. "And that's just what he wants," he said emphatically, "to keep the Jeep! No!" He turned back to Josh, catching a smirk on his son's face that quickly disappeared when he noticed his dad saw it. "Josh, you give me the keys to this vehicle right now."

Joshua looked at him, trying to decide if he should try to talk him into giving him the Jeep, but realizing he couldn't remember seeing his father this mad ever before. "Just give me a minute," he said, as if he was being pushed too hard while digging in his pocket for the key. "Here, take it," he said, as he took it off the key chain and handed it to his father.

Matthew looked at the key in his hand with a blank stare. His hand was frozen open. He just stared as he began to breathe slower, his face was still slightly red but the little vein on his forehead began to disappear. He looked up for a second at Josh, about to say something, but stopped himself. He looked at the car, rainbow roof, Pink Floyd symbol on the hood, and little holes in the roof leaking into the interior. The holes made him the angriest. He shook his head while looking at them dripping.

The others stood by quietly. They watched the people passing by, trying to stare them away from looking at them. Vickie was speechless. She had never seen Matthew, in all of Josh's vagary react with so much anger. She just stood with her purse hanging from her forearm, and her arms folded, watching.

Matthew looked back at the key in his open hand, while still shaking his head, and relented, "Josh, I just can't take this Jeep back," he said. "Here," he handed the key back to Josh, "Take it!"

A few weeks had passed since the Jeep incident in the church parking lot, as it had become referred to, and Josh came to the house once again, trying to get money from Vickie. This had happened so often that Matthew told Vickie she couldn't give him any more.

"I'm missing five hundred dollars I had in an envelope in my room," Vickie began, trying to head off his most likely persistence for more money. "Did you take it, Joshua?"

"Why do you always blame me?" he answered defensively. "You got other kids too, ya know!" Josh looked down at his hand for a moment where he held a torn-in- half piece of lined paper.

"I just think it's weird, that whenever you come over, things suddenly disappear," she said, getting up from the couch where she had been sitting. Vickie was tired. She was tired of Joshua always coming over stirring the pot, taking things and asking for a handout. "I'm just sick of you, Joshua," she cried out to him. "Why do you keep coming back here?" she continued. "Can't you see you're not welcome here!"

It was just about noon and Joshua knew the others would be at school. This was his favorite time to come over. He knew they'd be alone in the house and he'd have a better chance at getting money from his mom. "I knew you would blame me for the five hundred dollars," he began, while fiddling with the paper in his hand nervously.

"So you knew about it?" Vickie said sarcastically, "You magically knew. Hum!"

"Well I needed to use if for food and clothes," he said, "I have to eat you know."

"Oh, Joshua," she said, "You always have an excuse for everything."

"It was just a loan," he said back to her. "I have a loan document for you to sign." He handed her the piece of paper he had in his hand. "See, you just sign it and the loan is legal."

The torn in half piece of paper was hand written by Joshua, and made to look like a dollar bill. It had a face drawn in the center with a circle around it. There were some illegible words written on it with lines continuing from them as if to mean lots of words were there. The five hundred dollars was written clearly with a line beside it. "That's where you sign," Josh said as he pointed to the line.

"Oh, brother," Vickie said, with a sarcastic chuckle. "What do you expect me to do with this?"

"Luck O' the Irish!" Joshua said with a smile.

"We're not even Irish!" Vickie exclaimed. The anger set in. "Leave!" she said, pointing to the front door. "Just get out of here this minute!"

CHAPTER NINETEEN

Documented

VICKIE RECEIVED THE FIRST OF several letters from Joshua. She had gotten up with the kids for school, remembered she hadn't taken in the mail the day before, so headed out to get it. She could smell the freshness in the air as she stepped outside. It had rained the day before leaving a clean scent of flowering bushes and springtime. "It's been quiet around here lately," she thought. "Kinda nice that Josh hasn't come over for awhile." She smiled as she reached into the mailbox to get her mail. She began walking back, reading the front of each envelope. She got to one addressed to her, with a return address from *the White House*. "Josh," she said to herself shaking her head, "the White House?" She took a breath and opened the envelope. The letter was headed "GRANDMA AND GRANDPA" with, "ANTARTICAN MAJIC DOWNTO 15%" written letter by letter down the left side of the page. It was written on white-lined black paper all in pink ink. It began:

> "I SAW THOES AIRPLANES WITH NUKULEAR MISTLES. JUST LIKE THE WRIGHT BROTHERS, THERE FOR DECEMBER 17, 1903. WAS THE DATE IT HAPPENED. THEY LIVED WITH THEIR FATHER IN DAYTON, OHIO, ALEXANDER GRAHAM BELL. HE MUTTERED SOMETHING ABOUT ANOTHER FLIGHT IN 1898."

"Oh gol," Vickie said to herself. "Dare I bother with the rest?" She knew the answer to her own question. She walked up to her front step and sat while reading the remainder of the letter:

> "THIS VODO DOLL SHE WON OUT OF THE MACHINE HAUNTED ME ALL LAST NIGHT. SCARY LOOKING CLOWN IT IS. BE CAREFUL WITH THESE THINGS I TELL YOU BECAUSE I CARE.
>
> I WROTE A 10 PAGE "AWARD WINNING" ESSAY TO MY DOCTOR DAVE ABOUT MEDICINE, IF IT WAS A TEST IN SCHOOL I WOULD HAVE ACED IT. PHD. JOSHUA MITCHEM DOES SOUND NICE LIKE ICE.
>
> IN ARABIA, EGYPT, THE PYRAMIDS STILL STAND. ARE WE DOING OUR

JOB? HE WHO DESTROYS ONE IS CURSED AND HIS FAMILY IS LEFT WITH RETARDISM. WHAT IF WE HAD OUR ALAINS- ALIAS DO IT? THAT WOULD LEAVE OUT NAME COWARDS. SOMETHING I AM NOT WILLING TO DO." He signed the letter, then wrote it out "JOSHUA MITCHEM."

"He must be back at Spanish Peaks," she said quietly to herself as she got up from the step and walked into her house.

"Another letter?" Vickie said, taking the mail in a second time that day. It was so nice outside that the walk to the mailbox sounded good to her. She had only a few envelopes in her mailbox but on top of the stack was another letter addressed to her, with a return address of *Washington St. Fort Bg. #402*. She could tell it was Josh by the writing. The envelope was a little thicker than usual and Vickie was curious about what was inside. When she opened it she found several items enclosed with another letter. There was a two-dollar-off coupon for *Papa Murphy's*, that had been sloppily cut out, a two page *Medicare Summary Notice* that was addressed to Joshua, an overdue library notice from *The Pueblo City-County Library district*- addressed to Joshua, and a little white piece of note paper folded, with Josh's writing in ink, which said:

"-CCH FEDERAL TAX #8610TAX
BENEFIT FOR ALL WHO PERTISIPATED
ON THE SEPT. 11th 2001 IWC.
(1) NEW YORK CITY LIBERTY
BONDS
(2) LIBERTY ZONE
(3) 35,000$ BENNIFIT
(4) LIBERTY ZONE PROPERTY
(5) PROPERTY LEASE, 5 YEARS

At the bottom of the note, Joshua had written in pencil:

"HOW DO I COLLECT THE DEBT THAT
IS OWED?"

The handwritten letter on lined paper was folded with a paper on the outside entitled *Department of Veterans Affairs*. It was a blank form for a *Fuel and Heating Inspections Report* with a hand written note in pencil from Josh at the bottom of it stating:

"I SNUCK THIS OUT OF A LOCKED
FISILITY"

"Why does he bother sending this garbage?" Vickie said to herself, again sitting on the step on her front porch. She then began reading the letter which was headed:

"DREAM X3"

"Here we go again," Vickie said to herself, "He's documenting his craziness!" She continued to read:

"TEMPRATURE CHANGE IN THE 600MILE PER HOUR TRAIN, ANTARTICA; TEMPO. DROP FROM ABLE CREEK TO ZEBRA CLIFFS. TRAIN OF THE FUTURE IS APX ¼ AS FAST AS A NASA ROCKET. 108 FEET RETAINING WALL, TO 42 FEET GASOLINE SPACE. APX. THE SANFRANSISCO BART SYLIMAR. GOVERNMENT INVESTMANTS FOR WORK (MEXICANS) 200.00 $ EXP. 62.50 $ NON. EXP. JOB GROTH; GREIT/INCREASED GASOLINE PRICES; GOOD. TOLLS AND GOVERNMENT TAX IS A REGONAL COMPLAINT. GAS AND FUMES RADIATE 'ALAIN' PASSAGEWAY. CONSISTS OF A 42 FOOT COPER WALL, A 108 FOOT GAS VAPOR CREATING A OPPISITE OF VERTICLE 'HELIUM EFECT.'

TEMPRATURE CHANGE IN AFRICA TO ARABIA INCLUDES A HEAT 'PRESSURE CHANGE' VALVES WILL RELEACE RADIANT FUMES PILOT IS A TEST TUBE BABY! SO WHO CARES!

(PRESSURE + RADIANTX X VELOSITY /2) Eq(2)

(PRESURE + RADIANT X VELOSITY /2) Eq (3)

MY ANSWER IS Eq (3), EQUASION THREE BECAUSE THE TRAIN WILL

SLOW AFTER RELEASE OF DA GAS,
LOOSING THE HELIUM EFECT.
(PLEASE INCLUDE ME IN ON THE
INVESTMENT.)

"Wow!" Vickie said to herself, "Can he get any worse?"

Vickie skipped getting the mail the following day just in case there was another letter from Joshua. She had felt sick inside thinking about just how far from reality his thinking really was. She didn't even tell Matthew about them as her stomach ached just talking about it so she put the letters into a drawer in her nightstand.

"It doesn't seem like it is real," she said to herself while walking to her mailbox. She continued while shaking her head, "I still think it is a dream and I'll wake up one day and he'll be normal."

She opened her mailbox and there were two items in the stack from Josh. One was a post card addressed to himself with their address on it. It was plain white and on the back it was written completely in gibberish and signed by Josh. "Oh brother," she said to herself. She began to walk to the step as she opened the other thick legal sized envelope. She sat down on the step and began to go through the items inside.

"What?" she said to herself, "What is all this?" It contained a round cutout of an astrological chart from a newspaper and two two inched cut out oval-framed pictures, one of President John F. Kennedy and the other of Andrew Jackson. There was a cutout of a digital camera add, a postcard of the Mormon Oakland Temple, and a statement from the *Pueblo Community Health Center,* addressed to someone else. Josh had filled in the amount due with "810.00$" and wrote in the return corner:

WIDOW COOLEY-OFFICER MITCHEM
FRANK BOGART & FAMILY

Also included in the hodge podge of items were two *Sweepstakes Clearinghouse* vouchers for four hundred dollars, addressed to other people. This time, there was no letter.

Vickie sat in disbelief shaking her head. There were no more questions, just silence.

A few days had passed and Vickie had not received any more mail from Joshua. She had begun to develop an automatic ache in her stomach every time she went to get the mail. As she went through the pile each day, she began to feel a sense of relief when she had seen that Josh hadn't sent anything. "What am I thinking?" she asked herself. "I should be happy he sends me stuff. At least I know he's alive!"

It was the beginning of a new week and the kids were back in school. Vickie went out to get her mail and on the top of the stack was a letter addressed to her with a return address of "JOSHUA MITCHEM WASHINGTON EUROPE." Vickie held the envelope in her hand while walking back to the house. She sat on the step and thought, "O.K. he's alive and this is just the way it is.

Just open it and maybe there will be something of value inside."

There was a letter on lined paper inside to "GRANDPA, GRANDMA". Vickie began to read:

"THANK YOU FOR THE 10 CAR'S I DID RECIVE MY 2 FARARI'S. TO LOOK AND NOT TO TOUCH, REMEMBER? DONE-DONE, AS THE MURDER SONG GOES. MY NUCLEAR MEDAL HOWEVER IS NOT FOR SALE. I BRING THIS UP BECAUSE I WANT YOU TO BE PROUD OF YOUR GRANDSON. SOMETIMES I WISH I COULD SIT AT THE COFFIE SHOP AND WRIGHT MY DAILY LETERS IN GERMAN, AT A SPICIFIC TIME, BUT ACKIS NOSTIS DONDAS ASH-ASH MONDAS FOOLIS ISH. NO BUT I'M SHURE YOU UNDERSTOOD THAT PHRAISE. I GOT 30,000.00 IN THE BANK BUT IT'S MONEY FOR INVESTMENTS. THEY KNOW IT'S TIME TO MOVE AN SHE IT STILL WITHOLDING THE NOTE, IT IS LIFE OR DEATH IT IS DEATH, DEATH TO ANYONE WHO DOES NOT LISTEN TO ZERAHELMIA, MY MOUTAIN'S. CITY IN THE CLOUDS. THERE ARE NO BLACK'S THERE ARE ALIANS AND HUMANS."

He signed the letter, "JOSHUA MITCHEM."

There was a savings deposit slip enclosed filled out with random numbers. Vickie looked once again at the nonsense. "I can't believe it!" she said to herself. She thought for a moment and added, "I suppose I better! It's all in writing right in front of me." She began to massage her stomach, as it had been aching while she was reading.

CHAPTER TWENTY

Smokin'

"GIMME ANOTHER HIT, MAN," THE thin, unshaven, and scraggly looking young man said to Josh in a high pitched stoned voice.

Josh flicked his lighter and sucked another hit for himself then passed the clear glass pipe to the man sitting next to him on the couch. The T.V. was playing one of the *Friday the Thirteenth* reruns in the background and the living room was dark.

"Got any left in there for me?" Candy asked, looking at the scraggly man take a hit from the pipe. Using the light of the television, she held up a little baggie half full of white chunks of crack cocaine, looking to see how much she still had. She caught a scene from the movie and laughed a little saying, "Right on!" Candy was a well-dressed fake blonde. Her hair was styled with feathered bangs and hung long past her shoulders. She was chunky around the waist but managed to squeeze into designer clothing. Her nails were always done in bright colors, with little Rhine stones to sparkle and accent them. She wore her pointed dress shoes with spiked heels even while she was in her house. This night was no exception.

The man lit another hit for himself and then passed the pipe to Candy. "Thanks, dude," she said, taking the pipe from him. She tried to light the pipe and nothing lit up.

"Just put another piece in," Josh said, watching her try to light it. "You got tons," he said with a smile.

Candy laughed, and said slowly, while trying to open the baggie with her shaking hands, "I'm so buzzed!" She managed to open the baggie and pull out another chunk and put it into the glass pipe. After lighting the pipe, she sucked in another hit and as she blew it out said, "Damn this is good!"

"Hand it over here," the other man said, sitting on the floor wasted. He wore a baseball cap covering his mostly bald head with only long strands of greasy brown hair stuck out from the back edge of the cap. He had on no shirt or shoes and only wore loose old Levi blue jeans held on with a worn out brown leather belt.

"Not before I get mine," Josh said with a wink as his hand went out toward Candy, his new girlfriend. Josh was wearing his dirty Pink Floyd tee shirt, blue jeans which slipped half way down his butt, and his white tennis shoes. The two of them had just met in Spanish Peaks. Josh had been in again for another three weeks to get stabilized on his meds. He reached over to the floor in front of the couch where she was sitting. "Right, honey?" he said.

"You got it," she said. Just as she passed the pipe to Josh, the sound of a baby was heard crying. "Oh, I gotta get Ace," she said, struggling to push herself up from the ground and trying to balance herself in her spiked heels. Her two year old boy had been lying on her bed in her bedroom sleeping. She put him there before her friends came over and had forgotten he was there. As she finally stood up, little Ace came walking into the living room. His diaper was urine and poop soaked, hanging down under his butt. It swooshed as he walked, sending a strong old urine and rotten feces odor into the room.

"Damn," the man with the baseball cap said, "That little dude stinks."

"I didn't know you two had a kid," the unshaven scraggly man said. "Why'd you name him Ace?" he said with a chuckle.

Josh answered quickly, "The kid's hers. I never knew her before Spanish Peaks!"

"I thought you all was together before," the man said back. "When you was kissin' on her in there, it looked like you two was long time lovers!"

Josh laughed proudly. He always liked to get a girl while he was an inpatient. "They just like me. What can I say?"

Candy went into her bedroom and pulled a diaper out of the bag it had come in that she had stuffed next to a stack of clothes she had just ripped off from her favorite designer knock off store in town and went back into the living room.

"So, you didn't say why you named him Ace," the unshaven man said when she walked into the room.

"Ace Freely," she answered. "Ever heard of him?"

"Yeah," he said, totally wasted with his head falling backward onto the couch. "I think I heard a him."

"From Kiss, you know, the band."

Just then her thirteen year old son, Gene, came in from the front door. "Dude, where have you been?" Candy asked, almost as if she really cared. "You didn't take my car out again, did you?" she asked accusingly.

Gene had a habit of taking off in her car whenever he felt like it. He learned to drive because his mother was usually too drunk or too high to drive. He had become the designated driver. "Yeah, so what?" he snapped back, "Here's your keys!" He tossed them across the room to her, making a point of everyone in the room seeing him. He laughed and walked into his room, ignoring the party and closing the door behind him.

"Now, Gene," the man with the baseball cap on said. "That's an ordinary name. You name him after an uncle or somethin'?"

"Gene Simmons," Candy said, laying her baby onto the floor in front of everyone in the dark living room. She peeled away the tapes on the sides of the diaper and sloppily wiped down the yellowy-brown loose stool from his butt with the cleaner end of the diaper. She tossed aside the wreaking diaper and then she placed the new one under his butt with his little legs held up in the air with her other hand. "From Kiss," she said, sticking her tongue out of her mouth far, wiggling it like the singer at them. She then dropped her baby's legs down onto the carpet.

"Sick," Josh said. "What are ya gonna do?" he laughed. "Lick the diaper!"

"Woah, dude. Guess you like Kiss," the man with the baseball cap said in his stoned voice.

"Hell yeah," she said. "They're the bomb!" Candy answered while pulling each tape tightly, pressing into baby Ace's little hips to secure the diaper.

"Speaking of bombs," Josh said as he lit another hit from the pipe. He giggled. "One time I lit a old house on fire," he began. The men listened as best as they could considering they were so high. Josh got up and began pacing. He looked down as he said with thought, "Like no one lived there, so I put a flame under the curtains, man. They take off burning."

"You burnt the house down, dude?" the man on the floor said. "Dude, you're crazier'n me!" he laughed.

"First the curtains burned, then the kitchen," he continued.

"You better not be thinkin of doin' that here!" Candy said giggling also, as she gave her son a pat on the butt sending him away.

"Nobody wanted it anyway," he said breaking into a laugh. "So I ran outside to watch it burn, and when I got outside, a explosion happened inside." He laughed some more, "Like a bomb!"

"No lie?" Candy asked. She reached over to the man on the floor and lit another hit for herself.

"It really pisses me off," Gene began. "Every time I bring my girlfriends over, Josh starts hitting on them."

Candy was wiping beer off of the counter in the kitchen that had spilled from her friend's visit the night before. There were ash trays knocked over with cigarette butts mixed into the spill.

"What?" Candy said, scooting out the butts into a pile, not believing what she was hearing. She and Josh had only been together four weeks but she thought they were really good together. "I can't believe he would do that!"

"Well, he's always high or drunk, Candy," he said to his mom. "What do you expect?"

"Shut up!" she said. "He ain't either. Besides, just cuz some whore of a thirteen year old says a guy's hitting on her, you can't believe it!"

"Oh yeah!" he argued, getting offended at her remarks about his girlfriends. "Let me tell you what your little boyfriend does," he said mockingly. He liked to emphasize the fact that Josh was at least ten years younger than her by calling him her 'little' boyfriend.

"He grabs her right here," he pointed hard at his chest, "when she walks by him!" Gene was getting madder, moving closer to his mom. "How do you like that? He grabs little girls!"

"You seen 'em do it?" she asked, scooting the pile of the butts off of the counter and into her hand. She walked over to the trash can and dumped them inside.

Gene followed right behind her saying, "I sure as hell did!" He continued, "And, he asks them if they want some?"

"Shut up!" she said again. "Josh ain't that type of guy."

"Josh always laughs when they pull away from him," he said. "He thinks it's funny makin' 'em scared."

Josh walked into the kitchen, hearing the last part of the conversation. "What are you talking about?" he asked defensively. "I never touched one of your girlfriends!"

"Ah, come on, you cop a feel whenever they come over," he said turning his attention over to Josh.

Candy stood next to the sink wiping her hands onto a dirty dish towel. "You do that Josh?" she asked, giving her son the chance that he might be telling the truth.

"I can't believe you would believe that idiot!" he said, pointing hard at Gene while stepping in toward him, getting even madder.

Candy looked at her son. Gene had a tear welling up in his eye. She hadn't seen him cry since he was very little. "Get out!" she blurted out to Josh, trying to muster up the courage to really mean it and pointing toward the front door. "Get out of my house!"

Josh laughed. "You gotta be kidding!" he said, shaking his head. "You believe a thirteen year old and over a adult," he added ignorantly. She could almost see steam coming out of his ears as he filled with rage. He began walking toward the front door, punching a fist into the couch cushion on his way. Ace was sleeping on the cushion next to where Josh had punched. He startled briefly then fell back to sleep.

Candy began crying in the kitchen. "Look what you made me do," she said to Gene as she leaned back with her hands propping her along the counter's edge.

"Whatever," Gene said angrily. "He's a loser anyways!" He began to walk toward the living room.

Suddenly there was a loud crash heard with the sound of glass breaking, and then a dull "thud."

Candy pushed herself away from the counter as she and Gene ran into the living room where the sound came from. There was a red brick on the floor just under where Ace had been sleeping. Ace woke up crying, "Mommy, Mommy!" There was broken glass everywhere. Glass on the window sill, the floor beneath, the couch, and even on Ace.

Candy quickly ran to Ace, wiping off the few glass fragments that were on the front of his diaper and held him on her hip. She briskly walked over to the window and looked out. She could see Josh taking a last look at the window and then turning away walking fast.

"I'm calling the cops!" she yelled at him through the window. Candy quickly grabbed her cell phone and began dialing 911.

Vickie rolled over in her bed when she heard her cell phone ringing. She'd tried to sleep in, as she had gotten up early that morning to say good bye to Matthew before he left for the week. "Uh, hello," she said still half asleep.

"It's Candy," the voice on the other end said in a rush.

"Candy?" Vickie said, trying to wake herself. "What's wrong?" Vickie could tell by the tone in Candy's voice that something must have happened.

"They arrested 'im," she said. "I'm sorry, I had to call the cops."

"What for?" Vickie asked, snapping out of her sleep.

"He threw a brick into my front window almost hittin' Ace," she began with her voice quivering.

Vickie could tell she was genuinely scared. "What happened?" she asked with a caring tone in her voice. Vickie had become used to Ace coming over the past three or four times they visited. She loved children and felt sorry for Ace being in such a rough environment. Though Vickie didn't know about the drug use, she could see that Candy was lacking in her parenting skills. "Why did he do that?"

"He was pissed off about what Gene was sayin' about him," she said as she began to explain the whole story to her.

Vickie listened. After closing up her phone and setting it back onto her nightstand, she rolled back onto her side and began weeping.

Joshua began pacing back and forth in his jail cell where he was being held. He mumbled his gibberish, looking around with sudden jerky motions. He'd look at the floor, then the wall, then the ceiling and out the front toward the officers. They were just out of his view but he could hear them talking. "What are they sayin' about me?" he asked, looking across his empty cell at the wall. He saw the man with binoculars watching him as he paced. "Oh, you think I don't know you're there!" Josh said to him. He mumbled some more gibberish, and then said, "You were watching, motioning with his head back the direction of the officers, "You tell them the truth!" Josh began pulling nervously at his clothes. Then he began ripping them off, tearing his shirt into pieces. He walked over to his toilet and began stuffing the clothing into it, shoving them in as hard as he could, as if trying to shove his emotions with them. He then began pressing the flusher with his foot repeatedly, making a muffled flusher sound and causing the toilet to flood the jail cell.

An officer came over when he heard the toilet being flushed over and over again and took a look at Joshua standing angrily in his cell, naked in a puddle of stinky sewer water, with a freaky evil-looking stare in his eyes.

CHAPTER TWENTY ONE

Family Portrait

"JOSH, UH, HI," VICKIE SAID when she heard his voice on the other end of the line. She knew it had to be Josh since the caller ID didn't show a number when she opened her phone after the ring. Vickie had heard he was transferred from jail to the State Hospital in their forensic unit and had only heard from Josh once in the three months he had been there so far. He told her they arrested him for Vandalism as if it was a stupid crime.

"I get out in a week," Josh said. "They're finally coming to their senses!"

"A week? That must feel good." Vickie said, feeling awkward. She wasn't sure whether she was happy or not. It was good to hear from him, but at the same time, she wasn't feeling comfortable with having him around. "Where will you stay?" she asked with trepidation.

"The state has a place where I can go," he answered. "I get my own room."

"Oh, that sounds good," Vickie said with a sigh of relief, but wondering at the same time where the place might be. "Where is the room at?" she decided to ask.

"It's in town," he said. "I can walk to your place from there."

There was an awkward moment of silence. Vickie's feelings were essentially numb. The uncomfortable conversation then continued. Vickie couldn't understand her own feelings. One minute she was happy he called. The next minute she dreaded his appearing. She couldn't find genuineness in her attitude toward him. She searched for the right things to say, but they just seemed to come out wrong. "Walk here?" she asked.

"Camden, honey, go get your blue shirt. It'll look better with those pants," Vickie said, scooting him out of her room as she finished putting the last crease in Matthew's black slacks. She put the iron back up on end on the ironing board that was squished into their bedroom. "Honey, your pants are ready."

Matthew came into the bedroom from the closet where he had just sprayed his Musk and put on his long sleeved grey and black pin striped dress shirt. "Thank you, honey," he said taking it from her hands. "Are you sure you called Joshua to remind him of the appointment?" He began to put on the slacks.

"Yes," she answered as she let out a breath of air. Vickie had been busy running around all morning cooking breakfast and getting the kids ready for their family portrait. "I gave him explicit instructions and made sure he knew it was formal," she continued. "He said he had some dress slacks from a baptism he went to. It sounded like he knew what to wear."

The house was filled with the smell of freshly fried bacon. Vickie got up early to prepare a big family breakfast of scrambled eggs, bacon strips, hash browns, and homemade coffee cake and orange juice, thinking that if they were well fed, they would behave well. The night before she talked with each of the children, checking what they had planned to wear, making sure it was appropriate.

"Mom," Karley called from her bedroom, "Where is my necklace?" She had planned to wear her beaded necklace on a thin leather stand. She panicked thinking for a moment that Joshua may have taken it. "Never mind," she called out, "I found it."

Nathan sat in the living room dressed in his church clothes, wearing a pair of black slacks and a long sleeved white dress shirt and his black leather dress shoes. "Feels like we're going to church," he said under his breath as he rolled his eyes. "Don't we gotta go?" he asked, calling out towards his mom's room. "You said we have to leave by nine."

Kirstey walked into the room. "I can't go like this," she said grabbing a handful of her hair. "I haven't finished curling it yet."

"Well," he said to her, "hurry up! I'm not gonna sit here all day waiting for you!"

Vickie came into the living room, "Good, you're all ready," she said with a smile as she passed Nathan and went to the kitchen. "I just have to make sure I turned off the oven."

They were all dressed. "You have directions to his house, right?" Matthew asked Vickie.

"Yes!" Come on, let's go!" The boys and Vickie and Matthew piled into their steel-blue Grand Prix. The girls rode in Kirstey's car, checking their make-up as they hopped in. Vickie sat nervously in the front hoping Joshua would remember to be ready. Matthew pulled out of the driveway with Kirstey tagging along behind him and began down the road to Josh's new place.

It was Matthew's idea to have a family portrait made. He was proud of his family and began to realize they were growing fast and would soon be gone.

Vickie had jumped on the band wagon, making the arrangements with the studio and with Joshua. She bought the girls new dresses and the boy's new slacks. Putting them together in a photo was like putting the broken family back together. Joshua had caused so much pain and suffering to all of them. Now, as the children became older, their understanding grew. They began to see the family in the light of a purpose. Somehow this family would maybe give hope to another. Vickie saw this portrait as a coming together.

"Turn here," Vickie pointed toward the right. "I think this is it, over here."

Matthew pulled into a little alley next to a small red brick house. There was a white picket fence surrounding the front yard with portions of the fence falling forward and paint chipping off the short posts. The grass was not mowed, but was very long and green. It was scattered with dandelions and piles of dog poop. "I hope he's ready," Matthew said under his breath, as Vickie opened the passenger door. He understandably didn't have much confidence in Joshua.

Vickie knocked at the door. She waited about five minutes without anyone coming to the door. She looked back at the family waiting in the car, shrugging her shoulders at Matthew in question. She began walking around to the back of the little house when Josh suddenly walked out the back door. "Josh!" she said in a startled tone, "there you are!" She looked him over. She didn't know what to think, then asked, "Did you remember we were going to get a family portrait done today?"

"Yeah!" he promptly answered. "That's why I got dressed up!"

Not knowing what else to say and feeling rushed, Vickie just said, "Oh!"

They began to walk toward the car. The family sat waiting patiently. Josh was smiling and looking forward to seeing his brothers and sisters.

"Oh my gosh," Matthew thought as he looked at Joshua. "Somehow I knew this would happen."

"Hi everyone!" Josh said as he approached the car with his smiling face.

The other kids began to laugh under their breath. The girls tried not to be obvious about their reaction to

Joshua's appearance. The boys figured this was par for the course, but were entertained with how he looked. They all knew how important their mom had made this portrait out to be so they kept their comments to themselves.

"What should we do?" Vickie asked Matthew when she got to the car.

"Get in!" he said. He looked at her directly. He motioned to her to come in. "Come on," he said, "let's go!"

Vickie got into the car and Joshua squeezed into the backseat next to his brothers. "Where is the studio?" Joshua asked.

There was a deafening silence in the car. Everyone held their thoughts.

As I looked at the picture, a million thoughts ran through my mind. The family I grew to love and know looked so *together*. Matthew proud. Vickie strong. Kirstey and Karley beautiful young ladies with their entire futures ahead of them. Nathan and Camden, handsome young men, heading into their futures with confidence. And Joshua, well different. "Look at you," I said to Vickie, as I stared into the picture. "There is an expression on your face I have never seen before."

I had come a long way to visit my sister. I had also come a long way in my life. My four children were difficult much of the time but I never had to deal with something like schizophrenia. My life had taken many bumps and curves also. The only way I could survive the turmoils of life was through my personal faith in God. At times, I felt I had merely survived. Being successful, to me, was just that. Survival!

"What do you mean?" Vickie asked me as she joined me in looking at the picture.

"I can't quite put my finger on it," I said shaking my head. "There is a look of, I think, acceptance maybe." Nodding, I reaffirmed, "Yeah, acceptance, that's what it is."

"Wow!" she immediately responded. ""You nailed that on the head!"

"What do you mean?" I asked.

"Well," she began, "the day we went to have the picture taken I was really worked up. I wanted so desperately for everyone to look perfectly. You know, the perfect family thing."

"Yeah," I agreed. "I know."

"Well, when Joshua came out of his house wearing that," she pointed to Joshua in the picture, "I just about had a fit."

"Oh?" I asked.

"I just wanted them all to look proper, you know, the perfect Mormon family."

I just stood listening. My heart went out to her. I had so much pain with raising my children in their teens. I too dreamed of the perfect family. It didn't happen for me. My marriage had failed as I struggled to get my children through the roughest years of my life. I understood her feelings well.

"So there was Joshua in his bright tie-dyed shirt. All purple, blue, yellow and pink. He had on those white floods," she pointed to his pants in the picture. "Then, he wears his baseball cap turned sideways and his old tennis shoes!"

"It's just a picture," I thought at first. Then I saw the look in her face again as I stared deeper into the portrait.

"So, what about the acceptance?" I asked.

"Oh yeah," she continued. "That was big for Matthew and me. As we all sat in the car on the way to get the photo taken, we came to realize that this *is* our family. I know that sounds simple," she quickly added, "but I mean, we realized that this is what we have and it's O.K. with us. Our Heavenly Father had answered our prayers."

"The acceptance." Tears began to well up into my eyes. I had struggled for so many years wanting my family to be a certain way. I wanted success for them. I wanted bright futures with financial security. I wanted the American dream. But it didn't happen quite that way. My kids struggled to get by each day. Some did better than others. They were tattooed, pierced, and just what they wanted to be. I didn't feel so lucky, I guess.

I began to realize as I looked into my sister's family portrait that God had answered my prayers as well. My children were happy in themselves, being who they were, not what I expected them to be. Acceptance began to fill my being and a weight lifted from my shoulders that I had been carrying around for many years. I even began to wonder if we had turned out the way our parents had hoped. That concern too, lifted. Tears flooded my eyes as I turned to my sister and began hugging her. We held each other for what seemed like an hour.

"You know what?" Vickie said, breaking our embrace.

"What?" I asked.

"Remember how I used to light a candle whenever something special happened in my life when I was a kid?"

"Oh, yeah," I said quickly, "I remember you getting teased for it too."

"Yeah," she nodded. "Well, I kept doing that even when I left home and got married."

"Seriously?" I questioned.

"Yeah, I did." She continued. "But at some point I quit doing it." She thought back to when Patches was burned, sadness fell over her. Vickie's eyes welled up with tears. "And then," she said, breaking out of the sadness with strong conviction. "When the picture was taken I suddenly realized it was O.K." She looked at me, placing her hand on mine. "That Joshua was just who he was, and I couldn't change that."

I looked at her with compassion, holding her hand in mine, "It is O.K." I said, feeling it for me as much as I felt it for her.

"I went home that day and for the first time in years, I lit a candle." Vickie said to me softly, gently nodding with a smile.

"You did?" I asked, brightening with a smile also.

"Yes!" she said. "I felt free. The burden of trying to change something I couldn't change was lifted. It was a very special moment for me."

We stood together. Quietly. Amazed. We continued to look at the portrait, or maybe it was more than that.

Luck O' the Irish Limericks

An elaborate story was told,
'Bout a rainbow and a huge pot o' gold!
In a world of green,
All the wonders were seen,
By a lad whose reality had been pulled.

There once was a confused disheveled lad,
Who diligently sought to be glad,
With his spray painted cars,
And antennas to mars,
On-lookers considered him mad!

With a Bible he persisted to do,
A big job with colored highlighters too!
With earnestness the lad wrote,
On every word and every quote,
Though 'bout the meanin' the lad had no clue.

There once was a man with a chatter,
If German or Spanish, no matter,
He spoke aloud words,
That seemed too absurd,
But the curiosity from others left him flattered.

A dirt-filled dump truck was left with its keys,
And a confused young lad thought, "It's for me!"
So he hopped in the truck,
And with his amazing luck,
Drove around for a day 'fore it was seized!